A Woman of Grace and Strength

Lilliet Garrison

1

A Woman of Grace and Strength

Copyright © 2013 by Lilliet Garrison

Printed in the United States of America

Published by: *Wisdom Brings Freedom Ministries*

ISBN-13: 978-0615734408

Religion/Christian Life/Personal Growth

CONTENTS

Dedication

I dedicate this book to all the women who look to God to make them what they were created to be—beautiful in His sight!

1

SHE RECEIVES STRENGTH
THROUGH SURRENDER

"Fear not, for I am with you; be not dismayed, for I am your God; I will strengthen you, I will help you, I will uphold you with my righteous right hand." (Isaiah 41:10)

God wants you to thrive so you can lead a confident and optimistic life in an increasingly dark world. We become strong and secure when we surrender to God and let Him make us what we were meant to be. When we become what the bible calls "a peculiar people set apart," we shout to the world that we're different. This difference doesn't come to those who want to stay creatures of habit.

Most people want to gravitate towards what's safe and known, as the unknown makes them feel insecure and out of control. But settling for mediocrity actually draws vitality out of us and we become dull, unoriginal, and uninteresting as a result.

We often don't understand the reasons behind our restlessness. It's because we've chosen a lackluster, boring life rather than the growing, ever-maturing life Christ wants us to seek. We've allowed ourselves to become spiritually complacent. We've stopped "watching and praying" as the Lord warned us to do.

- Blessed is the one who does not walk in step with the wicked or stand in the way that sinners take or sit in the company of mockers, but whose delight is in the law of the Lord, and who meditates on his law day and night." (Psalm 1:1-2)

Peter, John, and James spent three years in ministry with Jesus as He diligently taught, mentored, and instructed them on what was to come.

Yet, for all His instruction to them they couldn't conceive that His time on earth was quickly drawing to an end. This single prevailing weakness—the lack of insight and understanding—became their downfall.

As the disciples sat down to eat with Jesus on the night of His arrest, their minds were preoccupied with many concerns. None of their concerns, however, were centered on His impending death. Instead of understanding His message to them, the disciples spent their time arguing over who among them would be the greatest.

Earlier in the day the disciples had been consumed by the details of the Passover dinner (Luke 22:10-13). When Jesus arrived at the upper room, no one offered to wash His feet, so He took a towel and began to wash the feet of His disciples (John 13:5).

Later, Jesus would reveal to them a starling truth: each of them would abandon Him that very night! Peter argued adamantly, "Even though all may fall away because of you, I will never fall away" (Matthew 26:33). None seemed aware of their own pride or lack of insight regarding the grave events Jesus spoke of.

As the evening continued, Jesus spoke about His betrayal. Yet His message didn't penetrate their hearts. They couldn't conceive of this evil thing happening to the One who changed so many lives and worked so many miracles in their presence. Since they couldn't perceive it, they failed to learn the most important principle for winning any spiritual battle—to *watch* and *pray.*

Even today, many live as the disciples did when Jesus' earthly ministry was near its end. They aren't prepared for what's to come. We get caught up in our everyday affairs. We fail to listen because our own dreams, passions, and needs take center stage.

Are you protecting your faith?

Perhaps the disciples pondered after Jesus' death if they could have done anything to prevent His arrest. Maybe they became fearful over what might happen to them as His followers.

Jesus gave us a powerful example of how to overcome both fear and evil. In the hours leading up to His death He demonstrated how to be victorious: *He surrendered His will to His Father's will.*

The disciples had this same opportunity for victory. This was a test for them. Would they be faithful in the last hours? They failed the test not once, but three times. Even in the end when they were told to watch and pray, they couldn't meet the challenge.

Perhaps you identify with the disciples. Maybe you've grown complacent towards spiritual things. Possibly, you've never truly considered that Jesus died to set you free. There's no need to feel condemned, for our natural "flesh" nature is inclined to focus on self. We're all prone to selfishness. By focusing our "spiritual eyes" we could see that Jesus has a better way for us to think and live.

Accounts of failure and success in the Bible are recorded for our instruction. We can learn from the disciple's failure by not falling into the same temptation to become spiritually complacent.

If life has beaten you down and others have taken advantage of you, take heart, for God's Word says you can draw from His strength and He'll cause you to rise up and be mighty. He'll restore to you what you've lost. God makes something beautiful come out of our tragic events.

As you mature in your relationship with Christ, you'll begin to see that your difficult circumstances served a purpose. We don't need to be thankful for hard times, but we can be thankful for what hard times produce in us. We must be after the "fruit" it produces. As a rule, fruit doesn't come during good times, for good times don't cause us to stretch and seek answers from God.

Difficult times serve to teach us what we need to know. They bring a new motivation and purpose to our lives. Often we can't conceive of a different life beyond the one we're currently experiencing.

We must adjust our feelings and thinking to what God's Word tells us is truth—not our *perceived* truth. We can only change our thinking when we let the Holy Spirit go to work on us with our full permission. When we think differently, according to God's Word, we interpret life in a whole new way.

Our life is like a wheel. When we adapt wrong thinking and practices, we become out of balance and our wheel doesn't travel smoothly. It can't move along smoothly unless it's in balance. When it is, there's no need to push from behind. It can pick up great speed, as it does what it was designed to do.

New thinking brings about new possibilities. Being transformed by God's Word gives us insight and balance. With proper balance we can move along life's path as we were intended to move—unencumbered. Being balanced produces a process in us:

1. We start to *visualize* a new life.
2. We have *expectations* of a better life with Christ out in the front leading us.
3. We're *motivated* to live godly, thriving lives that bless the Lord and others.
4. We begin to *meditate* on God's many blessing as we continue to submit our will to His plans for us.

With time we discover God has been faithfully leading us along our spiritual journey. He leads us into all truth. We thank Him for our difficulties, since they brought us to a greater awareness of our need for a Savior and Deliverer.

Darkness before the dawn.

Long ago, Bible prophecy foretold that world conditions would continue to deteriorate until the return of Jesus (2 Timothy 3–4). Jesus revealed that human efforts and ideas will eventually bring this deceived world to the *brink of annihilation*, and that "unless those days were shortened, no flesh would be saved; but for the elect's sake those days will be shortened" (Matthew 24:22).

Scripture tells us that Jesus will return to the earth as "Prince of Peace," to establish a world government from Jerusalem that will bring joy and harmony to the whole world (Isaiah 2:2–4; 9:6–7). He'll point all people to the one true God (Isaiah 30:20–21; Zechariah 14:16–20). At that time, the one "who deceives the whole world," Satan the Devil, will be banished from the face of the earth, and the *Kingdom of God* will appear (Revelation 20:1–2).

Jesus came so you could be prepared.

This is the time to be warned, a time to learn and grasp the "big picture" of what God is doing in His kingdom and how His plan will unfold for all eternity. We can be prepared by heeding God's warning to live for Him and not the deceiver Satan.

Watching and praying implies knowledge and understanding of what's to come. We'll not watch if we don't understand what we're to be watching for. We'll not pray if we don't grasp what prayer accomplishes and what we're to pray for.

- "Those servants are happy when their owner finds them watching when he comes. For sure, I tell you, he will be dressed and ready to care for them. He will have them seated at the table. The owner might come late at night or early in the morning. Those servants are happy if their owner finds them watching whenever he comes. But understand this, that if the owner of a house had known when the robber was coming, he would have been watching. He would not have allowed his house to be broken into. You must be ready also. The Son of Man is coming at a time when you do not think He will come" (Luke 12:37-40, NLV).

Those who watch and pray with understanding comprehend God's larger plan for people. Those who have their minds on simple, everyday matters of how they can get ahead in this world won't understand what's to come. They'll have no understanding that God has a reward for those who prove faithful to Him.

God calls us to pray. But there comes a time when we must *act* on what we've heard and learned. Reading His Word and praying for His wisdom, discernment, and guidance keeps fear away and encourages us to stand firm in our faith.

How do you handle difficulties and disappointments?

When we experience circumstances beyond our control, our first response must be to go to God in prayer. The victory for winning every battle is learning to fight with prayer, the Word, and by putting on the full armor of God. Only full surrender to the Lord and what He desires to do in our life will bring us victory.

Is there a problem in your life that's too difficult for you to handle? Remember, nothing is too difficult for the Lord. Our problems aren't too great for Him. He's not surprised by our weaknesses either. When we, like Jesus, only want to do the Father's will and have died to our own, we've passed God's test.

9

The value of weakness.

Whatever brings you to your knees in weakness carries the greatest potential for your personal success and spiritual victory. Paul wrote in 2 Corinthians "When I am weak, then I am strong." These words bring thoughts of contradiction. How can that be?

Scripture counters man's natural thinking and is ridiculous to people who function by the world's system of reasoning. We reason when we are weak, others will take advantage of us and we'll be in worse shape than before. We strive to stay on top by controlling others and our environment. All of us have experienced the stress that comes from trying to hold everything together. We may look like we're in control on the outside, but on the inside we're coming apart.

None of us can escape the pressures of life. Most of us know what it feels like to be hurt, disappointed, and even overwhelmed by the unfortunate paths our lives take. We know the sting of rejection, humiliation, and failure. Regardless of the level of control we may believe we have over our lives, there are always unexpected situations that pop up and catch us unaware. There are just some aspects of life that we must admit are beyond our control.

What circumstances are beyond your control? Is there a personal, relational, health, or financial need that you have? Remember in such times that in your weakness—Jesus is strong.

Weakness that works in your favor.

Our weaknesses are often the very thing that will get us to lay aside our pride and admit defeat long enough to call on the Lord for His help.

No one enjoys feeling weak, whether it's emotionally, spiritually, or physically. Apart from God, our natural, human spirit doesn't want to be dependent and can't stand the thought of being weak and vulnerable. But this is nothing more than our human pride at work. There will always be a gulf between us and the Lord when we hold on to our pride.

Pride resists the loving nature and calling of God. Prideful self won't tolerate being humbled, and this is the very thing God calls us to be (James 4:6; 1 Peter 3:8).

Just as weakness carries a great potential for strength, pride carries an equally great potential for defeat. It cannot co-exist with God's Spirit of love and humility.

 Humility moves us closer to the Lord, while pride keeps us separated from Him. That very separation is how Satan tempts you to rely on your own strength. Pride was Satan's downfall, and it's the one element that must be removed if we want to experience the peace that comes from an intimate relationship with Jesus.[1]

We're *called* to accept Christ's strength. Our strength is not within ourselves or our ability. It's in Christ who strengthens us. (Philippians 4:19).

Since we'll never be able to eliminate all trails from our life, it's important to respond properly to them. We can blame God, others, and even ourselves. We can become depressed, bitter, resentful and hateful. Or we can give up control and let the God who's all-wise direct our lives as He knows best.

This is not a passive surrender, but a surrender that comes by acknowledging that He has the better plan and knows us better than we know ourselves. His plans for us are always good and not to harm. He wants us to succeed and will make every provision for it. But it comes by His timeline and in *partnership* with Him.

God wants the glory for doing something miraculous and spectacular with our lives. If we concede to His plans, we'll enjoy an enormously profitable life that brings Him glory and brings others love, tenderness, compassion, and ministry.

There's true value in acknowledging our weaknesses before the Lord. He blesses us beyond measure when we do. We see His loving kindness and mercy when we allow Him to have the place He desires in our life. He created us for Himself. Consequently, He's a jealous God and He won't share us.

Weakness has the ability to bring you to the end of yourself. It's there you realize your need for someone greater. Only Jesus can calm the storm that is battering your life. He's the One who gives you the wisdom needed to stand firm and to resist temptation.

When we accept our weaknesses and admit that we don't have all the answers to life's many perplexities, God goes to work on our behalf. He sends encouragement and protection and helps us problem-solve difficult situations. He gives us the needed creativity to do what He's leading us to do. The Holy Spirit is the power source to do what is beyond our own natural ability.

To prosper in all areas we must seek excellence, fruitfulness, and passionately desire to have Christ change us and make us dynamic. This requires surrendering our desires and leaving behind our complacent ways. This is how we find fulfillment. We must take success as our rightful inheritance. We must desire *more*. The Lord will satisfy the heart that is hungry for Him and no others.

Are you weary? Has running after worldly success and wealth exhausted you? Are you afraid others will see your weaknesses and think less of you? Is there a failure in your life that could expose your deepest flaws and wounds? Let it go. Release your frailty and fears to Jesus who loves you unconditionally. Let Him strengthen you and put His loving arms around you. Nothing compares to the freedom that waits for you when you surrender your life to Christ.

Living life to the full.

Although surrender takes first priority, obedience and commitment are two key principles for spiritual and personal success. When we submit our lives to Jesus we're indicating by our action that we're willing to follow His lead. What does it take to follow a leader? The desire to obey his instructions! Through training and knowledge of God's directives we can be obedient.

Military forces are taught to respect authority and to obey commands. They start by going through basic training to understand the importance of commands, authority, and obeying with little information.

If a soldier doesn't understand instructions from his commander, he'll soon wander into enemy territory and may lose his life. Good commanders give clear and concise commands. They train their soldiers to *listen* and *obey* their orders, as obedience preserves their life.

The soldier's role is to fight the enemy! He must learn how to stay alive long enough to conquer his opponent. He fights with a mindset to win, to conquer, to overcome, and then rule. Soldiers are *trained to win*. Losing is not an option, for it brings captivity or death. The front line is not the place to ask questions or to consider if being obedient is fitting.

God left us His Word. It contains His instructions to us. When we follow His lead, obey His instructions, and remain in His territory—we preserve our life. God's Word teaches us how to deflect evil, stand strong, and remain victorious. When we lay our human desires down, recognizing we have the most excellent Commander to get us through life victoriously, we'll submit to His authority and rule. When we respond to Him in obedience, He ensures our protection and triumph.

Submission is only a difficult command when we don't understand that life is a battleground. When we think we have the better plan, we'll not obey or submit to a higher authority.

We're called to function as God's soldiers. We have an enemy who wants our total destruction. We must so acquaint ourselves with God's Word, His written battle plan, to know when He's speaking to us and telling us where to turn to avoid annihilation. This is how God protects us. We must train ourselves to be obedient to His commands to experience victory.

Facing difficulties is part of our basic training. When well trained, we'll not hesitate when the command is given to get out of the way, to pray, or to run. When we understand the purpose of difficulties, we willingly submit to God.

We can trust every instruction that comes from our Lord. Unlike human leaders, Jesus never makes a mistake, nor does He grow weary or irritable with us. His statutes are always for our advancement and protection. If we wander away from Him, He'll allow us to hurt just long enough for our willful nature to be broken. This pain has a purpose. It gets us to the place where we'll submit, as a sheep does for the shepherd, for it holds a greater reward. We can trust the true Shepherd's leadership, commands, and plans for us.

Our season of adversity usually doesn't need to be any longer than we determine. If we're excessively prideful, that period may take some time. But if we learn to submit swiftly, our hardships can pass without undue delay. Passing Christ's tests toughen us to win every battle. When we're broken and weak in our own power, Jesus makes us beautiful and useful for His service.

Just know that not all trials are a result of sin. Some certainly are for we may reap what we've sown. When we determine to go a way that's contrary to God's, there's peril. But some trails come to strengthen us and make us fit for God's service and kingdom. Submission to Jesus is not a sign of weakness. It's a sign of holy allegiance and immense internal strength and power. God's goal is for you to be weak in yourself—but *strong* in Him.

Living the blessed life.

How do we access all the good things God has for us? The answer: we must not shun any opportunity God gives us to be obedient. Perhaps He's asking you to lay down your worldly ambitions to pursue what He has for you. Perhaps He's asking you to reach out to someone in pain, or to leave your present city to go to another nation as He did with Abraham. Maybe He's asking you to give of your financial resources to a group of people.

God is the source of all our abilities and blessings. We're able to work with our minds and hands to earn a living. When we're mindful of His many blessings to us, it's not difficult to comply.

A changed focus lets us get excited about the possibilities God has for us. The fact that God will include us in His global, superior plan is an awesome thought, one that is both humbling and thrilling at the same time.

God is willing to speak to us when we quiet ourselves long enough to listen. When we ask Him what plans He has for us each and every day, we're living as He instructed the disciples—by *watching* and *praying*!

2

SHE SEEKS TO BE
EMOTIONALLY MATURE

"For the Lord sees not as man sees: man looks on the outward appearance,
but the Lord looks on the heart."

(1 Samuel 16:7, ESV)

G od sees you through His eyes of love. He created you because He loves you and wants to enjoy you. He also wants you to love yourself as much as He loves you. In fact, He wants *you* to see yourself as He sees you!

If you feel you don't come anywhere close to loving yourself the way God loves you, know that He isn't looking for you to change yourself before He'll accept you. God declared that everything He had made was "very good," and you're not going to be His first exception.

David gives us a glimpse in the book of Psalms of how God views us.

- "I praise you because I am fearfully and wonderfully made; your works are wonderful, I know that full well. My frame was not hidden from you when I was made in the secret place. When I was woven together in the depths of the earth, your eyes saw my unformed body. All the days ordained for me were written in your book before one of them came to be." (Psalm 139:14–16)

- But the Lord said to Samuel, "Do not look on his appearance or on the height of his stature, because I have rejected him. For the Lord sees not as man sees: man looks on the outward appearance, but the Lord looks on the heart." (1 Samuel 16:7, ESV)

These Scriptures reveal how God sees you and how intimately He knew you before you were born.

God looks upon the heart of people, while we tend to look at our appearance. God sees what we're made of, our substance, our essence, while we look at the form or outer shell.

God gave us our appearance and emotions. Those emotions, which were invariably good and positive before the fall of man, now give us different messages. God made us complex and our emotions are part of that complexity. Emotions are neither good nor bad.

God, the Holy Spirit, and Jesus all have emotions. In the Old Testament we read that God became angry with the stubborn Israelites for their continual disobedience and ingratitude toward Him. Moreover, God didn't allow Moses to enter the Promised Land because of his fury in striking the rock with his rod, rather than speaking to it as God had commanded.

We know of Jesus' emotions during his human lifespan from his visible grief at the tomb of Lazarus, to his righteous anger at the moneychangers who were desecrating the temple courtyard. The Holy Spirit, we're told, groans on our behalf as He intercedes for us with the Father.

In our natural condition, before we're transformed by God's truth, we often believe what the enemy says about us. That's the "truth" we tend to hold in our heart. But it deflates and defeats us.

If we don't know how God feels about us, we stake our lives on our perceived truth—even if it runs counter to God's truth. What's more, "the truth we believe" determines how we view our circumstances and the world in general.

Although it's God who gave us our emotions He doesn't want us to be governed by them. Our emotions are often unreliable and our perceptions skewed. We're stimulated by pain or pleasure. Emotions are designed to move us in a certain direction, spurring us to take action or to make a decision.

If the underlying emotions are inaccurate, we may be moved to make negative decisions. Far from being harmless, these negative emotions have a destructive quality that can alter the whole course of our life. It's only when we let the Holy Spirit guide our emotions that we can be moved in a positive direction.

God created you: Body, soul, and spirit.

Your soul manifests itself in three areas: your *mind*, *will*, and *emotions*. God intends for people to be in continual fellowship with Him, to be guided by Him through *relationship*. It's our emotions that allow us to feel the love He has for us. Without them we wouldn't be able to love Him in return or understand the concept of love.

Although Adam and Eve severed intimate fellowship with God through their rebellion in the garden, they retained their God-given emotions. Through rebellion their emotions lost their inherent positive quality and became a destructive force working against them.

God never intended for our emotions to rule us. Only close fellowship with God can gain us back the control we lost. We get into trouble when we allow our feelings and passions to take over. When we don't understand that God created us to master our emotions, we'll let them master us. Our best efforts at trying to understand how we're wired are faulty. It's God who gives us understanding, knowledge, and wisdom into His purposes for us.

Our emotions fuel our passions. Passion, like fire, can be a blessing or a curse. Fire purifies and gives us light and warmth, but if misused it will destroy and consume. Uncontrolled fire leads to destruction. Lust is uncontrolled and unrestrained passion, passion fueled by Satan to consume and destroy.

Like fire, emotions can move us to love or destroy. Positive passion fuels God's purposes for us. Only when we permit the Holy Spirit to invade us are we able to live a restrained and balanced life. God's prescription to reinstate our equilibrium is love. While lust brings us death—love brings us back to life.

The word—thought—feeling association.

The way we think and speak determines the course of our life. Our thoughts and words are influenced by what's in our heart and mind. We learn by hearing, so what or whom we listen to, the messages we receive and repeat, shape and mold our future.

- "For as he thinks in his heart, so is he." (Proverbs 23:7, NKJV)

If you take the time to listen to your own words, you'll discover a surprising connection between what you hear and say, and what you *believe*. The words you speak are seeds that produce either a positive or a negative harvest in your life. Negative words produce negative thinking and vice versa. Negative thinking also produces negative feelings, which in turn lead to negative decision making.

Scripture tells us to guard our heart from ungodly people and influences. Compulsive behaviors such as anger, lust, overeating, overspending, and a general lack of self-control can enter our lives through ungodly associations.

- "My son, pay attention to what I say; listen closely to my words. Do not let them out of your sight, keep them within your heart; for they are life to those who find them and health to a man's whole body. Above all else, guard your heart, for it is the wellspring of life." (Proverbs 4:20-23, NIV)
- "For by your words you will be acquitted, and by your words you will be condemned." (Matthew 12:37)

When we speak poorly about ourselves, we feel condemnation. That's because we learn by repetition. We come to believe what we say over and over again, either as self-talk or in conversation with others. Our continuous repetition reinforces these thoughts and cements them into firm beliefs.

We counter self-condemnation when we actively take steps toward overcoming insecurity and disapproval. You replace negative beliefs about yourself with positive affirmation by simply repeating Scriptures that declare God's thoughts about you. God's Word is truth! Therefore, His thoughts about you are true.

Any negative pattern can be turned around by replacing it with a positive one. Repeating Scripture is a positive practice that will alter your view of both self and of others.

You may not be able to control all of the negative influences that affect you, but you can control your messages to yourself. You can bring good into your life by believing that the words you speak impact you. You have more control over your tomorrows than you realize, but it'll take more than knowledge of this principle to change your life—it'll take *action*!

Jesus used Scripture to counter Satan's attacks.

Jesus coped with all of the emotions and temptations that we do. Though fully God, He was also fully man. Jesus was tempted by Satan in the desert when He was especially vulnerable from extreme hunger and exhaustion after fasting for forty days and nights. Even in His weakened state, Jesus countered Satan's attacks by quoting the Word of God. The Word was His shield of protection. When we speak the Word of God over our lives, Satan can't penetrate the barrier.

When Satan hears God's Word—all he can do is flee. The devil can't stand Jesus or His powerful Word, and that makes Scripture the very thing we can and must use to deflect him. Jesus treated Satan and his numerous distractions as a mere annoyance. Satan isn't going to stick around if every word from our mouth speaks of Jesus' power. The enemy has NO power unless we give it to him. If we don't know the Word, or how to appropriate its power, we're in effect giving him authority to rule over us.

Jesus was ridiculed, spit upon, tempted, and persecuted. He experienced hunger and fatigue, just as we do. Yet, He didn't give in to doubting emotions during difficult times. He overcame the evil one with the use of His Father's Word. He knew too, what His Father had sent Him to earth to do. By taking His rightful, legitimate authority, He restored intimate, personal relationship between man and His Father once again.

Jesus controlled the encounter with Satan in the desert. In fact, through all of His earthly encounters with the enemy, He defeated Him at every turn. When we deploy the methods Jesus used for victory, we'll come out strong and victorious too.

Anger management is possible with God's help.

YOU—through the power of the Holy Spirit who resides in you—are the one who controls your destiny. Not Satan or those who would wish to do you harm. God commands us to take control of our emotions, and failing to do so is disobedience.

Perhaps the single most problematic emotion with which we deal is anger. This is a subject widely covered by biblical authors.

- "A fool vents all his feelings, but a wise man holds them back. . . . Do you see a man hasty in his words? There is more hope for a fool than for him." (Proverbs 29:11, 20)

- "Be angry, and do not sin." (Ephesians 4:26)

Anger is not always sinful. We get into trouble when we yield to the temptation to react to this emotion in a negative, self-defeating manner.

- "Be slow to wrath, because the wrath of man does not produce the righteousness of God." (James 1:19–20)

Not all anger is forbidden. The text doesn't tell us never to be angry, but cautions us to be *slow* to anger. The problem with anger is what it leads to. Many other passages refer to "self-control" as an essential characteristic of Christians. Every passage that commands self-control is focused on the issue of controlling our tempers (1 Corinthians 9:25–27; 2 Peter 1:5–8; and Galatians 5:22–23).

God understands our human frailties and our temptation to believe we can't change, so He never asks us to change ourselves. He only asks us to surrender our will to His, to make possible our transformation. Eventually we'll be able to say with confidence, "I can accomplish whatever God commands me to do." Since God will never command the impossible, He makes the impossible, possible.

- "We do not face any temptation that is beyond our ability to handle, including the temptation to lose our temper. God will make a way of escape." (1 Corinthians 10:13)

Prepare yourself for Satan's attacks.

Lust, like anger, takes many men and women down the wrong path because they fail to understand how Satan operates. Look to the area of life in which you're most tempted; almost without exception, you'll find that it's the very area in which you're already the weakest.

We can overcome our weaknesses by handing them over to God and asking Him to help us. The Christian's life is about growing into spiritual maturity. Ask God to help you restrain and discipline your natural nature, to reflect more accurately Christ's nature. This is asking in agreement with what the Lord wants for you. It's the mark of a mature Christian.

People who accomplish a great deal have learned to focus and discipline themselves. A sign of someone who remains immature or ineffective is that they're unfocused, unrestrained, and unable to check their natural impulses.

When we strongly desire to mature, we become aware of behaviors that are keeping us stunted. The Holy Spirit helps us to modify our thinking and behaviors to reflect our Christ.

At some point everyone gives in to seduction and wrong thinking. When this happens, we're failing to cast down wrong thoughts and imaginations by harnessing the power of God's Word, as Jesus did.

- "We demolish arguments and every pretension that sets itself up against the knowledge of God, and we take captive every thought to make it obedient to Christ." (2 Corinthians 10:5)

When we cast down vain imaginations and high thinking we're refusing to allow Satan an inroad into our mind and heart. Let's not forget that Satan has a purpose for us too. If we won't permit him to enter, he can't steal from us or derail our ultimate purpose.

It's urgent that we anticipate and identify Satan's attacks and acknowledge our vulnerable points, the chinks in our armor. Ask God to strengthen you. Meditate on God's Word *slowly*, chewing and digesting it into your very being. Continually remember His promises to care for you. Repeat Scripture often to stay on track. Do a study on spiritual warfare to acquaint yourself with Satan's practices. When you learn to identify demonic attacks for what they are, they'll no longer take you by surprise.

We have a tendency to believe that oppression and addiction are "issues" of life with which we must inevitably struggle. But they aren't issues at all. They're the works of Satan. We must call them what they are if we're to recognize them as Satan's work to destroy us.

Christians are the prime target for Satan's attacks. He wants nothing more than for us to abandon our promised destiny. Satan first strikes our emotions, then our thinking and will. When these become distorted our perceptions of truth becomes distorted too. We must stop his advancements.

Woe to us when we put more confidence in our feelings than in God's written Word. Fear, worry, anxiety, and depression are the results of allowing Satan to defeat us through our emotions. When we're depressed we lose interest in life in general and, more particularly, in spiritual things, including our relationship with the Lord, His Word, and His people. This must not be tolerated! We must become angry enough to rise up against Satan's attempts to influence us.

Resolve from today onward to become aware of how Satan has deceived you and taken from you in the past. Ask God to make you strong to resist. Become a student of His Word and you'll have a shield to protect you.

Anger turned inward becomes depression.

Depression is actually anger turned inward. This connection is not usually well understood.

When we refuse to abide in Christ, we're tempted to go our own way. The farther away we move from God, the more Satan fills our mind with his thoughts. Taken to an extreme his thoughts are focused on impending doom, death, suicide, perversion, eating disorders, cutting, etc. With his negative thoughts and emotions, darkness soon settles over us. Our heart grows cold. We become morose, moody, withdrawn, and inclined in one way or another to harm ourselves or others.

Many fail to understand that some forms of depression have demonic roots. Since many physicians aren't Christian, they don't move beyond human education and solutions. Psychology is man's wisdom, based on human reasoning and learning. Its man's best attempt to understand the human condition, but it isn't God's methodology. We weren't created to be in a continuous state of anger, worry, or discontent. When we turn from our empty human philosophies to receive Christ, the answer to our flawed condition, we receive joy, rest, and a sound mind.

The antidote to fear and depression.

Gratitude and worship directed toward our God, who loves us beyond measure, dispels evil thoughts and harmful deeds. God longs to give us a sound mind and a peaceful countenance. This is the effective and perfect medicine for what makes us sick.

Any evil tendency is a part of the "old man," the old nature. It's with us until we accept Christ as Savior and turn from it. Only when Christ is at the center are we finally freed from this continual destructive bent.

The Bible tells us from childhood on that the human heart is filled with evil.

- "The Lord saw how great the wickedness of the human race had become on the earth, and that every inclination of the thoughts of the human heart was only evil all the time" (Genesis 6:5, NIV).

- "The Lord said to Himself, I will never again curse the ground because of man, for the imagination (the strong desire) of man's heart is evil and wicked from his youth; neither will I ever again smite and destroy every living thing, as I have done." (Genesis 8:21, AV)

When we turn from our old ways and turn to Christ, who makes us new, evil is banished. This is indeed *good news.*

Your estimation of yourself matters.

Having a correct view of yourself and accepting the value God places on you determines if you're capable of ***receiving*** from Him. How much you receive, determines the degree to which He can heal you. God desires to heal, but He can't do so against your will.

Believing in Him and His ability to turn your life around for good is putting your trust in Him. In response, He makes you both worthy and able to receive the good He has for you.

Obedience is key. It demonstrates your confidence in His ability to change you. But you must work to believe it. By speaking what God says about you, you internalize His truth. His truth fills you with positive thoughts, emotions, and attitudes that are in alignment with His purposes for you. In this way you are working *with* God, not against Him.

Experiencing God's love drives out fear and insecurity.

We're able to succeed at being our true selves when we first experience God's love towards us. God is the initiator of love, as He *first* loved us. When we permit Him to love us, we're able to reciprocate His love.

- "We love because he first loved us." (1 John 4:19)

- "The second [great commandment] is this: 'Love your neighbor as yourself.' There is no commandment greater than these." (Mark 12:31)

Unless we understand the implications of accepting Jesus, not only as Savior, but also as Lord, we're in danger of rejecting Him. When presented with salvation we tend to think of what we must give up, never considering what we have to *gain*. Jesus came to heal us and make us whole, physically, emotionally, and spiritually. Refusing Him means we're refusing our wholeness and healing. It isn't enough to have heard that Christ loves us; we must internalize His love through firsthand experience with Him. When we diligently seek Him, God rewards us with His love by overwhelming us with and in it.

- "And without faith it is impossible to please God, because anyone who comes to him must believe that he exists and that he rewards those who earnestly seek him." (Hebrews 11:6)

God created each of us with an innate craving for intimacy, a longing that can only be filled by accepting His love. He wants us to long for Him as much as He longs for us. Too often we're at a loss to identify that "God-shaped void" in us. Our longing for God is inborn, planted there by the Creator Himself. It's there to lead us to Him.

- "I in them and you in me. May they be brought to complete unity to let the world know that you sent me and have loved them even as you have loved me" (John 17:23).

You can't exhaust God's love for you.

Don't make the mistake of thinking you must overcome your flaws and shortcomings on your own, or that God is tired of hearing about your seemingly endless problems. Know that you can't wear God out or convince Him not to love you any longer by your dependence on Him.

God is love (1 John 4:8), infinite (boundless or measureless) love, love that can't possibly be depleted. Love isn't something He does; it's *who He is*. It's His very essence.

God desires nothing more than our total surrender giving ourselves to Him to change and transform as He wishes. When we agree to leave behind our prideful self-sufficiency, we give God the go-ahead to do His astounding work on us. The prophet Zephaniah makes this point beautifully, picturing us as helpless babes capable of doing nothing beyond being loved.

- "He will take great delight in you, he will quiet you with his love, he will rejoice over you with singing." (Zephaniah 3:17, NIV).

We are God's personal handiwork, His pride and joy. God took great pleasure in creating you and His investment in you will continue, unabated, through all eternity.

Are you a grasshopper or giant?

The book of Numbers recounts that Moses sent twelve spies into the Promised Land to scout it out and report back. Ten spies returned with a defeatist report and two with a positive assessment. Ten of twelve were fearful of the giants they had seen in the land. The enemy had easily convinced them that those giants created an insurmountable obstacle. They were already defeated in their minds for they believed what they saw, rather than the God who could change all things in their favor.

- "We saw the Nephilim there (the descendants of Anak come from the Nephilim). We seemed like grasshoppers in our own eyes, and we looked the same to them." (Numbers 13:33)

The ten spies returned home *defeated* because of how they saw themselves. They had a negative self-image. Believing themselves weak, pitiable, and puny, their thinking produced in them their perceived reality.

The minority report.

- "Then Caleb silenced the people before Moses and said, "We should go up and take possession of the land, for we can certainly do it." (Numbers 13:30)

Caleb, one of the two spies who had gone with God, had a conquering mindset. He perceived no limitations despite seemingly overwhelming odds. He was confident because his eyes were on his sovereign Lord. He *believed* God. God told His people to go in and take possession of the Promised Land. Caleb recognized God's voice and responded to it with unquestioning obedience. Of twelve men, only two responded with faith and a positive report.

It strikes me that the percentages from this ancient story are a pretty accurate reflection of the society in which we find ourselves. Of all the people who profess to know the Lord, relatively few listen attentively really believing what He so clearly tells us in His Word. They may believe *in* God, but they don't actually *believe* Him.

When most people confront a negative situation they immediately give way to doubt and fear. Instead of looking to the Lord to see how He will make them victorious, they look to themselves, and lacking His empowerment, are reduced to despair and defeat.

Succeed at being yourself.

God will use us as we are. He equips us to overcome our weaker areas.

- "But God chose the foolish things of the world to shame the wise; God chose the weak things of the world to shame the strong." (1 Corinthians 1:27)

You don't have to be something or someone you're not. God will mold you into what He wants you to be. Your job is to believe Him.

When we believe God's good report, we overcome the negative self-image of our past. By believing what we *will* be (the giant), rather than what we currently see (the grasshopper), we become positive like Caleb and enter into our Promised Land.

- "We even saw giants there, the descendants of Anak. Next to them we felt like grasshoppers, and that's what they thought, too! (Numbers 13:33, NLT).

The approval that counts.

As believers we find our identity in Christ. This means that we see ourselves as separate from the world. God made each of us to be unique, a one-of-a-kind masterpiece. Don't squander your distinction by trying to be like anyone, or everyone else.

Ask yourself: "What does the world possibly have that I want or need?" A short list of its offerings: depression, anxiety, shattered relationships, greed, lust, debt, and poverty. Bear in mind that others are likely to be impressed by you only as long as you can do something for them. God the Father was impressed by His Son Jesus, and He accepts you without reservation based on Christ's merit.

Living with a confident, conquering mindset will keep you from crumbling under criticism. Learn to expect, and, yes, even to welcome disapproval. The world has always hated Jesus. It hated Him when He walked the earth and they hate Him now. Many hate us *because* we're Christians. We must learn to accept that this is part of taking up our cross daily. It's not personal, even though you may believe that it is.

We must develop a tender heart and a thick skin. Not the other way around. Unless I'm around other Spirit-filled believers, I *expect* others to reject my message. This perspective keeps me from being offended personally by their rejection. What they're rejecting is the message I'm bringing, not necessarily me.

If you're never rejected because your message is offensive, the likely explanation is that your witness is anemic. Yes, we can have a strong and powerful message without being offensive. We can speak the truth with a smile on our face and with tenderness in our tone.

People who are merely religious will reject the true message Christ came to deliver. They don't have the heart of Jesus. Many of them experience the same problems the world does. We must become strong in Christ to know beyond doubt what we believe and why.

Has it ever occurred to you that God may be bringing opportunities for criticism your way? God could be doing so to bolster your faith and resilience, as these opportunities come to us as a *test*. Will we cower in fear, or proclaim in confidence that Jesus is Lord and no other can take His place? You know you're in a beautiful place when you no longer care what others think, but only long for Jesus' approval. Criticism is generally an indication that you're being transformed into Christ's likeness and becoming less like the world. God is never critical of you, so it really matters little that the world which is in opposition to Him, thinks less of you.

- "For God did not send his Son into the world to condemn the world, but to save the world through him" (John 3:17, NIV)

Your unique gifting and purpose.

The Holy Spirit has given all believers spiritual gifts. Find something you like to do, and do it well. You have natural talents that coincide with your temperament, but in addition the Holy Spirit gives at least one spiritual gift to all who accept Him. These special, "over and above" gifts equip the saints for the work of Christ.

Even if two believers have the same spiritual gift, they won't carry it out in precisely the same manner. Our background, education, family, experiences, and other individual factors predispose each of us to carry out our work for the Lord in different ways. Each of us is an original.

Ask the Holy Spirit to show you what you're good at. There's never any need to copy others, since the Holy Spirit has equipped you for what He has purposed for you. If you want to understand this topic further, I urge you to study the topic of spiritual gifts. One excellent website is: *Church Growth Institute/www.churchgrowth.org.* Os Hillman offers numerous studies, training programs, and mentoring tools, as well as single and group spiritual gifts assessments.

It's never too late to identify your spiritual gifts and the purpose God intends for them. God wants you to discover your purpose, the reason He created you. When you feel He has given you a word, do what He tells you. If you aren't sure, talk it over with a mature believer or pastor who can guide you. God wants you to be blessed, joyful, and fulfilled in His service. Discovering your purpose will bring you joy, pleasure, and great excitement.

Think back to the Old Testament story of Joseph and to the agonizing trials and waiting he had to endure before his purpose became evident. Many fall away for lack of endurance. They may not discern that when they hear from God it may take many years for everything to fall into place. Every Christian must go through this "conforming process" before they're mature and ready to handle their assignment.

Through the Holy Spirit's work we become less self-focused and less likely to seek glory for ourselves. At this place we're capable of giving ourselves to others and positively influencing their lives. Remaining faithful during our conforming process ensures that we reflect Christ and not ourselves.

Practical applications for attaining emotional maturity.

Let's summarize the characteristics that describe an emotionally mature woman. A definition of such maturity (you may already be familiar with it): The art of living in peace with that which we cannot change, the courage to change that which should be changed, and the wisdom to know the difference.

Such a woman…

1. Is composed and purposeful.
2. Has well-defined values and goals.
3. Copes with pressure and crises in a peaceful manner.
4. Is patient, determined, and capable of enduring hardship.
5. Controls her anger and settles differences tolerantly and logically.
6. Is humble, joyful, and compassionate toward others.

Take a few moments to assess your typical emotional reactions and how they affect others. New behavioral patterns must be learned and developed. This requires a change of attitude and direction: from a state of taking, to a state of giving. When we allow God to transform us, He renovates our heart. This transformation is characterized by godly wisdom, inspired problem-solving, right decision making, and the self-discipline that's made possible by controlling our emotions.

Emotional maturity doesn't anesthetize our emotions. It frees us up to fully accept and experience our God-given feelings and passions while guiding and controlling them.

Plan now to grow in emotional maturity.

Determine your weak areas. Set goals and guidelines. Establish checkpoints for reevaluation along the way. Don't be discouraged when you occasionally slip. Concentrate instead on the things you do right and the many instances in which you achieve mastery. This will help you to gain confidence, pick up momentum, and eventually reach fulfillment of your goals.

Emotional maturity includes developing love to its fullest extent—to the point that it becomes our chosen response. The apostle Paul summarizes emotional maturity in his affirmation of the power of Christ-like love in the life of a believer.

- "Love is patient, love is kind. It does not envy, it does not boast, it is not proud. It does not dishonor others, it is not self-seeking, it is not easily angered, it keeps no record of wrongs. Love does not delight in evil but rejoices with the truth. It always protects, always trusts, always hopes, always perseveres" (1 Corinthians 13:4–7).

Some manifestations of emotional immaturity.

1. Fearful of many things, including change.
2. Insensitive to and inconsiderate of others.
3. Whiny, complaining, moody, and demanding.
4. Overly focused on self: health, looks, relationships, problems, and issues. Unaware of others' feelings.
5. Intolerant of others' weaknesses, yet easily offended and accusing when hers are pointed out.
6. Competitive, demanding to be first in everything; not a gracious loser.
7. Argumentative, contrary, and aggressive. Needs to be right. Is a trouble maker, not a peacekeeper.
8. Impetuous, self-indulgent, impatient, compulsive shopper, no delayed gratification skills.
9. Sarcastic and cynical of life in general.
10. Always joking; unable to be serious, level-headed, or sober.
11. Disorganized, disheveled, distracted. Foolish and reckless in decision making.
12. Unable to concentrate. Irresponsible and unreliable as a result.

Do you know what you want from life?

If you've never stopped to ask yourself what kind of life you want, don't be surprised if the life you've accepted is disappointing.

A necessary first step in assessing our goals and plans is self-examination. If you find negative and immature emotions in yourself, and you will, don't be overly discouraged. Just acknowledge these concerns as areas that still need growth. Begin by asking some hard questions and being realistic about your goals. If you don't have objectives in mind now is a good time to change that.

Ask yourself:

1. Do I have peace and security?
2. Am I stable or volatile?
3. Do I like myself and enjoy my own company when I'm alone?
4. When I'm with friends, do I enjoy closeness with them?

5. Am I able to rejoice with them when they have good news to report, or do I find myself feeling secretly jealous?
6. Do I make excuses for my behavior or rationalize my emotionalism?
7. Do I convince myself that other family members have similar responses, thereby excusing inherited traits and bents?

Be aware of your emotional triggers; then discipline yourself to take control over your feelings and reactions. Keep in mind that you can come to understand yourself better by seeking the standards set in God's Word. Eliminate fault-finding introspection and the negative thoughts that Satan wants to plant in your mind. Keep your focus on what God says to you in His Word. This is the path to greater peace and emotional stability.

Learn to identify your true feelings and call them what they are— anger, resentment, jealousy, hatred, malice, etc. Don't be afraid or ashamed to examine your feelings. Keep in mind that the *renewing of your mind*, to which God's calls you, is the first step toward more positive thoughts and emotions.

If you're experiencing negative emotions because you don't know God, or don't know how to change your negative attitude or disposition, then ask God to come into your heart and make you new now. Ask Him to take out of you what shouldn't be there, and to instill in you those traits that will make you a secure, steady, and peaceable person. Be sure to cooperate with Him; you don't want to hinder your progress.

If and when you identify problematic actions, behaviors, and attitudes, ask God's forgiveness and then search out the cause. This will require honesty on your part. Look at and deal with your problems from God's point of view, spelled out in His Word, rather than from your human feelings, even though this will seem more natural to you.

Most women, when asked why they feel a certain way, are likely to answer "I don't know;" as they've never invested the time it takes to examine their own underlying motives. Being passive in this regard is itself immature. It indicates a failure to accept responsibility for how you react to situations and to others. If you tend to be emotional, don't conclude that just because you're a woman, it's your prerogative to spout off or lose control. Emotion isn't male or female and God calls each of us to be self-controlled.

Cause is important. If you truly don't know or understand the source of your negative emotions and corresponding behaviors, ask the Holy Spirit to reveal this to you and help you eliminate these destructive patterns. Be willing to change what the Spirit reveals to you by His grace and mercy.

Emotional maturity will come with God's guidance. It's one of the benefits that come from being His child. Balanced, healthy emotions are a part of the well-being God has promised to those who love Him.

3

SHE DEVELOPS GODLY CHARACTER
AND KNOWS HER TRUE WORTH

"Many women do noble things, but you surpass them all. Charm is deceptive, and beauty is fleeting; but a woman who fears the Lord is to be praised. Honor her for all that her hands have done, and let her works bring her praise at the city gate" (Proverbs 31:29–31).

The book of Ruth holds out hope to the hopeless. It's a love story for sure, but moreover it reveals practical aspects of daily life with all its cruelty, disillusionment, and setbacks. Love, loyalty, kindness, integrity, and devotion stand out. It contains profound spiritual truths, but none more important than that God desires to be our ultimate redeemer.

The lesson taught is although there is chaos in the land, meaning and fulfillment could be found by returning to simple truth—that no matter how bad things may be goodness can exist if we're willing to trust God with our life.

Ruth provides a beautiful example of a woman of dignified character, virtue, and loyalty in the midst of exceedingly difficult times. The account is set in the period of the Judges before the birth of King David. It's the story of how Naomi, her husband, and their two sons emigrate to Moab during a famine in Israel. In this foreign land the sons marry Moabite women. Mahlon marries Ruth, and Chilion marries Orpah.

In time Naomi's husband Elimelech dies, as do both sons, and Naomi decides to return to Bethlehem in Judea. Noami tells her Moabite daughters-in-law to stay in Moab, to return to their families and marry again. Orpah eventually agrees, but Ruth refuses to leave Naomi and accompanies her to Bethlehem.

As the story continues, we observe Ruth gathering barley in the fields of Naomi's relative Boaz, who shows special concern for her. Later, at Naomi's suggestion, Ruth hides in a shelter in the field until Boaz falls asleep and then quietly lies down by his feet (this was a custom of the time, a way for a woman to indicate her interest in marriage). When Boaz awakes, Ruth expresses her desire to marry him according to the custom of the kinsman-redeemer. But Boaz tells her that another man, a closer relative, has first right of refusal. At the city gate the other relative renounces his claim and Boaz marries Ruth. The end of the book relates Naomi's joy at this turn of events and lists some of Ruth's descendants, including King David. [1]

What we can take from Ruth's example.

The book of Ruth shows us a story of God's grace in the midst of very difficult circumstances. Ruth's story occurred during the time of the judges; a period of disobedience, idolatry, and violence.

We become fascinated with the characters of Ruth, Naomi, and Boaz in this unfolding drama, but God is the primary performer in this report. While all the players are free to choose their own actions, God's hand directs events to accomplish His purposes. Naomi's sorrow and emptiness are transformed into triumphant joy, and Ruth is rewarded for her commitment to Israel's God with an enduring place of honor in its heritage.

In Boaz we see a foretelling of the redemptive work of Jesus Christ. Ruth has no ability on her own to alter the affairs of her life. She's a picture of the absolute helplessness of humanity without a savior. Boaz's uncompromising agreement to pay the full price to redeem Ruth foreshadows Jesus' complete payment for our redemption.

If the most effective teaching is by example, then Ruth's choices teach us how to live. The example for us as Christian women is this: even in times of crisis and deepest despair, God will work His purposes through those who choose to follow Him faithfully. No matter how dark and hostile our world may become, there are always people who will follow God. He will use anyone who is open to Him to achieve His purposes.[2]

Ruth enjoyed a rich future and inheritance based on her wise choices.

When Ruth made the decision to stay with Naomi, she was in effect choosing Naomi's God. Her decision was uncommon, which made her reward uncommon too. Ruth exhibited her true character. Her attributes of loyalty, commitment, faithfulness, responsibility, and selflessness, revealed a young woman of surprising maturity and reliability. In fact, she stands in biblical history as one of the prime examples of a woman of substance.

Ruth showed uncommon wisdom by choosing Naomi over her own relatives. Commitment to her mother-in-law achieved for her much more than she lost. The decision to remain loyal to the one who had been so kind to her opened doors for both women. Upon their return to Judah, Ruth managed to find work, humble as it was, during a difficult time. She found new friends and eventually a new husband. Incredibly, God included her, a Moabite woman adopted into the family of Israel, in the line of Christ. The child she bore from her marriage to Boaz became the great-grandfather of David and therefore, in the lineage of the Messiah.

Ruth exemplified loyalty, integrity, and honor.

Ruth's story illustrates the triumph of courage over adverse circumstances. She chose character and wisdom over the familiar and comfortable and reaped a storybook ending to an earlier life of difficulty. Ruth was poor, a foreigner, and a woman, all signifying clear disadvantage, but she was encouraged by an older woman to overcome the obstacles she faced. Ruth had the wisdom to listen to Naomi's advice, and in turn, the bereaved older woman was blessed by Ruth's unfaltering loyalty.

The character and example of Ruth have special significance for us as Christian women. The story doesn't elaborate on her early influences, but we can benefit from her modeling of godly womanhood and character. Ruth remained committed to doing the right thing and God surprised her by meeting every need of both women. Her example teaches us that when we allow God to make us into the right person, we are in time led to find God's right person for us.

God blesses those who strive to be right (not as in winning an argument, but as in internalizing His principles for righteous living). We are made "right" through our relationship with Christ. When we seek to do what's honorable in God's sight, God blesses the work of our hands. Character precedes conduct. Faithfulness precedes fruitfulness. Responsibility precedes results.

- "But seek *first* his kingdom and his righteousness, and all these things will be given to you as well." (Matthew 6:33)

The story of Ruth reminds us of two truths.

1. God moved on behalf of Ruth and rewarded her for her character.
2. God will accomplish His purposes in the end, even if He chooses to use unexpected individuals, circumstances, and methods.

Ruth was unique for several reasons.

1. She had character that was uncommon.
2. She sensed something special about Naomi and wanted to know Naomi's God for herself.
3. She revealed a teachable spirit by listening to her wise mother-in-law and doing as she instructed.
4. She possessed a pleasing disposition, loyalty, and responsibility.
5. She had a strong work ethic, gleaning without complainingly every day in Boaz's field.
6. She had a strength of character that garnered Boaz's attention.[3]

Ruth and Orpah were still young women with a future ahead of them. But the kind of future would be determined by the life-altering decision they faced there on the dusty path with their foreign mother-in-law.

Ruth made the momentous decision to leave her past behind. Surely her family and friends would have provided comfort in her grief and most likely introduce her to a new marriage prospect. Having another husband would have allowed her to raise a family of her own. But the comfortable, complacent, logical choice wouldn't be Ruth's.

It started with one "right" decision.

What made Ruth chose the road less traveled? Why did she make a decision that would surely be hard on her, opting for a future unknown and uncertain?

Ruth was willing to leave everything behind to pursue what she sensed would be a better future. Ruth recognized, despite Naomi's admitted bitterness, that the older woman had something she herself lacked; a relationship with the living God. Ruth yearned to know Naomi's God and was blessed beyond measure for her decision to follow. That one right decision determined her ultimate outcome, legacy, and eternal inheritance.

Ruth was single-minded in purpose.

Ruth meeting her redeemer Boaz, especially in contrast to her challenging earlier life, represents the restoration brought to us when we wait patiently for the right thing. Ruth could have done the "normal" thing, but instead she made the wiser, "unnatural" choice.

The stories in the Bible always point us to our *Redeemer* Jesus Christ. We may have had a difficult earlier life, but by making the "one" right decision to follow Jesus, we join ourselves with the only One who can change our future.

Jesus is our Boaz—our Redeemer. He emancipates us from the faulty thinking that has produced a life of loss and suffering. He releases us from the sin which holds us captive, and offers us all-embracing freedom instead. Our Savior and Lord is beautiful to behold. We must cherish the treasure we've been given. Why would we do other than make the decision to turn from what holds no lasting value, to follow Jesus, who waits to be our sole remedy.

PRACTICAL APPLICATION OF CHRISTIAN CHARACTER
How to gain Christian character as Ruth did.

If you're a new believer, understand that your old patterns of behavior and thinking will gradually cease to fit. As the Holy Spirit reveals new realities to you, you'll discern a detachment with your past.

If you're sensitive to the Spirit's mentoring, you'll begin to identify ungodly traits that will hinder your spiritual growth and keep you from achieving what God has planned for you.

Be sure to implement everything the Spirit reveals to you about your new life. Determine to be obedient to His internal leading. Little by little, with His guidance, you'll become strong enough to leave your past behind.

- "Do not merely listen to the word, and so deceive yourselves. Do what it says." (James 1:22)

The fear of doing anything untried and unknown may have hampered you in the past. But now, as the Lord reveals new information to your heart and mind, you can safely let go of your old ways. He'll teach you to trust Him in your new life.

Spend the bulk of your energy pursuing this new life of yours. Become obsessive about it, pursuing Jesus with your whole heart. Become passionate about Christian character and where it will take you.

Replace the needs you've left behind.

Before coming to know Christ as Savior, many of us were passionate about the things of this world. Determine today to exchange those interests and attractions for the *better* things of God.

Be careful not to mix elements of your old life with the new. If you don't pull away from earlier loyalties—by the renewing of your mind by the Word of God—you may be lured back into your old lifestyle despite your good intentions. A measure of understanding, wisdom, and knowledge of God must be firmly rooted in us before we can clearly see that our former life was one of emptiness.

Keep your past—past tense. Instead, set your sights on the good future God has planned for you.

- "Set your minds on things above, not on earthly things." (James 1:2)

Embrace your new life in Christ. This may mean having to let go of familiar but unhealthy friendships. It may mean abstaining totally from your old routines and hangouts. Eventually, you'll have no desire to return to the things you've left behind.

Many of us find fulfillment by engaging in activities with people who share similar interests. A new life demands new thinking, new people, and new interests. We won't succeed in the new, while holding on to aspects of our former life. At best this is an attempt at behavior modification or psychology, and it comes from self, not from the Holy Spirit changing us from within. We can't be successful in any venture by merely refraining from doing something. Lasting change will come only when we've been renewed from within. Outward change is never sufficient. It isn't lasting, because it's modification not *transformation*. Christ is the only One who's in the transforming business!

We can replace those lost sources of fulfillment with new, better activities, social contacts, and behaviors that meet our "new" needs as a believer. Until your mind has been renewed with the knowledge that comes from God's Word, you aren't going to be strong enough to resist the old allures.

Don't believe you must isolate yourself, as Satan wants to convince you that you must give up everything to live for God. Isolation is the very thing that could lead you to return to your old ways. Exchange old behaviors that no longer fit the new design of your life with new and better ones. In time you'll come to love your new life and your new, true friends.

Wisdom will affect your future habits.

Asking God to reveal what new habits need to be formed will direct you to new contacts and opportunities. Ask the Holy Spirit where you should go to church, whom you should befriend, and what activities you should engage in. Be careful not to become too busy in *doing* – as the spiritual life is deepened by spending *quiet time* with the Lord. Only in periods of undisturbed intimacy, can we receive from Him what He wants to give us.

God will reveal things to those who spend time with Him and who seek more. But it doesn't come easily to those who are always busy or who habitually place themselves in busy, distracting settings.

Reading God's Word for guidance, direction, and insight clarify the transformation process. Also, reading positive Christian testimonies, books, and devotionals invites the Holy Spirit to transform our mind.

- "Consequently, faith comes from hearing the message, and the message is heard through the word about Christ." (Romans 10:17)

Going to church to hear godly preaching builds faith. Being part of a small group, or engaging in group Bible study allows you to hear Scripture, including testimony of how others have grown in their faith. All these methods contribute to the transformation of our old self into the new. Be sure as well to watch Christian programming and listen to Christian radio programs while you drive.

Be careful how you relax in the evening when you're tired. The temptation to watch mindless or immoral programming will bring the world back into your life. You'll need to fight the temptation to let the world have access to your eyes and ears. Perhaps you'll need to turn off the TV and tune out the world's music, opting instead to read a Christian book that will place the Word of God before your eyes. Listen to Christian praise music and let it minister to your spirit.

All of these methods and more serve to shut out the world, particularly once we enter the sanctity of our home. Make this your quiet place to pursue all things godly. This method completely transformed my life, and the Spirit will see to it that it works for you as well.

A woman of grace has a character that reflects God's character.

The book of Proverbs contrasts two opposite roads we can take in life—the road of *wisdom,* and the road of *folly.*

The word *character* can be applied to someone's nature, quality, temperament, personality, disposition, spirit, or makeup. When we're describing someone's character, we usually do so by recounting their attributes or characteristics. We may describe either positives or negatives—their strengths or weakness, or their morality or lack thereof.

Our true character has been said *to be who we are when no one is looking.* A person of good character has attributes that reflect God's, who is absolutely good and moral. Our negative characteristics, in contrast, reflect the enemy's attributes.

A woman of wisdom and character is also virtuous.

The "Proverbs 31 woman" is a woman of wisdom and virtue. We can learn what Christian character looks like by studying her. And we can examine her character traits to identify what it was that makes her so rare and valuable. We can discern the quality of her life by observing the wise choices she made.

- "The wise woman builds her house, but with her own hands the foolish one tears hers down." (Proverbs 14:1).

She's that "wife of noble character," depicted in the sayings of King Lemuel, an ancient wise person of unknown origin or background. (Proverbs 31:10–31)

- "A wife of noble character who can find? She is worth far more than rubies. Her husband has full confidence in her and lacks nothing of value. She brings him good, not harm, all the days of her life. She selects wool and flax and works with eager hands. She is like the merchant ships, bringing her food from afar. She gets up while it is still night; she provides food for her family and portions for her female servants. She considers a field and buys it; out of her earnings she plants a vineyard. She sets about her work vigorously; her arms are strong for her tasks. She sees that her trading is profitable, and her lamp does not go out at night. In her hand she holds the distaff and grasps the spindle with her fingers. She opens her arms to the poor and extends her hands to the needy. When it snows, she has no fear for her household; for all of them are clothed in scarlet. She makes coverings for her bed; she is clothed in fine linen and purple. Her husband is respected at the city gate, where he takes his seat among the elders of the land. She makes linen garments and sells them, and supplies the merchants with sashes. She is clothed with strength and dignity; she can laugh at the days to come. She speaks with wisdom, and faithful instruction is on her tongue. She watches over the affairs of her household and does not eat the bread of idleness. Her children arise and call her blessed; her husband also, and he praises her: 'Many women do noble things, but you surpass them all.' Charm is deceptive, and beauty is fleeting; but a woman who fears the Lord is to be praised. Honor her for all that her hands have done." (Proverbs 31:10–31)

Seven virtues of a wise and discerning woman.

1. *She is rare. Rare* means uncommon, not easily discovered. She's one among thousands, or "one in a million." The Proverbs 31 woman was rare because she lived with wisdom and diligence. She was *virtuous,* and this made her unusual. If virtue made her extraordinarily valuable, we can conclude that living without virtue

41

makes one, at best, common, or run of the mill. What is it, specifically, that makes us valuable?

2. ***She fears the Lord.*** Having the fear of the Lord doesn't imply that this model woman was afraid of God, but that she highly respected God and what He can accomplish in and through an obedient heart.

Wisdom leads us to recognize, hate, and run from evil. It keeps us from becoming prideful, arrogant, and full of ourselves. Wisdom leads us to be grateful by recognizing and acknowledging who it is that provides for and blesses us.

When we're cognizant of the source of our blessings, we naturally want to share this good news with others. Wisdom leads us to make wise choices and to be a blessing to others. It prevents us from going down a road that will lead to our destruction; the natural consequence of making poor choices. Proverbs 1:7 points out that the foolish don't simply ignore, but ***despise*** wisdom and discipline.

A virtuous woman, on the other hand, is full of the grace and wisdom of God. If you recognize that you've made poor choices that have led to foolish living, do as Proverbs says: Seek after godly wisdom. In response, the Lord will straighten your crooked path and add blessings to your life. Bear in mind that a different roadmap is always just one decision away.

3. ***She values her relationship with the Lord:***

She rises early in the morning. By spending time with the Lord while it's yet early, her day is ordered with right priorities. She seeks the Holy Spirit as her guide, consequently limiting time wasted on things of little importance. Her motives toward her family and others are pure since she's free to love as Christ loves. This liberates her from excessive negativity, anger, resentment, and bitterness. Her countenance is cheerful, her demeanor inviting. She's productive and multiplies her resources.

She's obedient to her Savior and Lord. Her intimate relationship with the Lord keeps her humble in spirit and beautiful in His sight. A woman who pursues the Lord won't spend her time chasing worthless things. She won't be drawn to potentially toxic people and relationships. If she's married, she looks for like-minded, mutually edifying friendships.

4. ***She is trustworthy and honest.*** A wife who can be trusted with confidences is rare indeed. Many women, when talking to friends or others, reveal personal confidences that have no business going outside their marriage. Such intimate matters aren't to be revealed to others. To share personal information about one's mate undermines the marriage and dishonors the spouse. This isn't building your house but tearing it down with disrespect. An honoring wife holds confidences and protects those entrusted to her care, responding with kindness, loyalty, and intercessory prayer. Her husband and children can be respected in the community because she doesn't bring them shame or harm.

5. ***She possesses godly virtues.*** Her dress and behavior are modest, pure, and chaste. She's dignified. She develops the "fruit of the Spirit" in her life: fruit that produces such desirable traits as patience, loyalty, tolerance, and love. She's moderate and restrained, never extreme in opinion and statement. She's confident. Confident that wisdom is of infinitely more value than fading beauty. Dignity is her true beauty.

6. ***She's strong and devoted to her work.*** She's an astute business-woman who contributes resources to her household. This doesn't necessarily mean a godly woman must feel obligated to work outside the home while she has young children in her care. If she's able to stay at home during her children's formative years, she's creative in managing the family finances, finding inventive ways to be thrifty or to bring in income while working at home, where she can remain the primary influence in her children's lives. Many women save money by shopping carefully and learning to be content with their home, hobbies, church activities, and families. Excessive shopping and spending reveal that emptiness has crept in, and lack of purpose leaves us wasting our valuable time and resources. Developing a ministry and interest in others will often alleviate this condition.

Augmenting our income can come in many ingenious forms. Learning how to creatively prepare nutritious meals on a budget, mastering sewing and finding fashionable clothing at high-end thrift or consignment shops are all rewarding endeavors. She's able to care for others because she busies herself with multiplying what she has. She isn't prone to idleness (laziness) or gossip. She guards her words and speaks well of others.

7. ***She seeks godly friendships.*** Solomon advised us to be careful regarding unwise friendships, cautioning that we eventually take on the characteristics of the people with whom we surround ourselves. We find numerous biblical cautions on this rule of bonding, among them:

- "Walk with the wise and become wise, for a companion of fools suffers harm." (Proverbs 13:20)
- "Do two walk together unless they have agreed to do so?" (Amos 3:3)
- "Do not make friends with a hot-tempered person, do not associate with one easily angered, or you may learn their ways and get yourself ensnared." (Proverbs 22:24–25)

Only a rare man is capable of discerning a woman of value and rarity.

Only a godly man can appreciate or recognize a woman whose countenance has been changed by God. Nabal, married to the beautiful and gracious Abigail, was a foolish husband who failed to discern the extraordinary treasure he had in her. The name *Nabal* means to disgrace, dishonor, lightly esteem, come to nothing, make vile, or wither.

Because Abigail understood that she had a fool for a husband, she approached King David to keep him from acting on his wrath over Nabal's ungracious conduct (1 Samuel 25:2–20). Upon Nabal's death David recognized Abigail's uncommon wisdom and value and took her as his wife.

In Ruth's case, the nearest kinsman didn't discern her qualities as Boaz did. Boaz had no doubt heard the talk about how good Ruth was to her mother-in-law. He could discern that she held the qualities that make for a valuable mate and an able mother.

In the story of Esther, Haman was a deceitful and manipulative menace to the palace and to the Jewish people. He never discerned Esther's wisdom and had no idea she was related to the very man he hated, Mordecai. Haman's lack of recognition of Esther's value led to his early death.[4]

A Proverbs 31 woman requires pursuit.

Many young women today mistakenly believe they've been liberated from yesterdays moral constraints, allowing them to pursue their chosen man. They think nothing of calling a man first and asking him out on a date, or declining to demand that he treat them with honor and dignity. They don't expect to be sought after, picked up at their front door, have the car door opened for them, or to have him pay for the meal and entertainment on their date.

Being rare means understanding not only our own value, but that the nature of a man includes the *art of pursuing*.

Proverbs is full of advice to young men about avoiding the snares of evil and temptation. The prostitute and her behaviors are common and always have been. She stalks a man with her provocative behavior, speech, and sexual aggression. She's anything but ladylike, poised, or gracious, having only her sexual attributes to tease and attract.

Unfortunately in our modern culture, too many young women have taken on some of these behaviors and mannerisms, not fully understanding the message they're sending about themselves and their worth. Sadly, this invitation easily piques the interest of a man who can never be faithful or honoring. These women don't understand the proper way to go about attracting someone of worth who will value and respect them.[4]

Not understanding true femininity and significance will cause you to sell yourself short. It was God's design to make woman feminine; and in doing so, complementing man's masculinity. Femininity is a gift, a commodity worth prizing highly. When we give it away freely and immediately, we're throwing away our gift and treating it as refuse.

If you didn't grow up with a good role model or someone who spoke value into your life, you might have taken on the values depicted in popular culture. They're propagated through TV programming, movies, women's magazines, romance novels, reality television, and tabloids.

Sadly, what's shown isn't going to get you what you really want, someone who'll honor and love you unconditionally.

The Proverbs 31 woman gets her understanding of true femininity from God's Word, not from the world. She's aware of her distinction and value, so she won't settle.

Anything of real value must be worked for. Jacob had to work for Rachel for 14 years. He wasn't willing to walk away from what he wanted and loved. If a man is unwilling to work for and appropriately pursue a woman, he isn't worth having. A woman of high esteem identifies these traits immediately in a potential mate.

Boaz had to **return** for Ruth. Ruth didn't pursue Boaz, but demonstrated quiet elegance and humble dignity, traits that attracted a good man.

David had to **send** for Abigail. She didn't approach him to ask whether he might want her for a wife. She let David pursue her because she understood her value to him.

The Persian king had to **choose** Esther over all the other beautiful maidens. He recognized something rare and valuable in her. She didn't spread the word that she wanted to be chosen above the others. She let the king develop a desire to have her based on her worth and distinction.

Each of these situations required the man to take action to reveal his intent. And each of these men offered a commitment and followed through with marriage and its benefits.

These women didn't settle, nor did they deprive the men of the art of the pursuit. They waited to be pursued by worthy suitors who recognized their assets. [5]

What do you want?

If you're unmarried, ask yourself what it is you truly want in a mate. Do you want just any man, or a godly man?

If you want a godly man, you need to develop the virtuous character to attract one. Anyone can have what Ruth received by seeking the God who gives good gifts. A woman of godly character, who knows her true worth, is rare indeed.

"The successful woman is the average woman, focused."

4

SHE DEVELOPS A GENTLE
AND PEACEFUL COUNTENANCE

"Rather, it should be that of your inner self, the unfading beauty of a gentle and quiet spirit, which is of great worth in God's sight."

(1 Peter 3:4)

Is it really possible to live a life of gentleness and peace in an aggressive and hostile world? Is it a fantasy to believe we can nurture a joyful countenance when everything and every-one around us seem to contribute to our stress level?

No, it isn't a fantasy, and yes, you can come to a place of perfect peace amidst what seems to be absolute chaos. But you must first understand that peace isn't something that just *happens* to you—it's something you *cultivate.*

The world has many philosophical and medical therapies for stress. Stress often becomes so intense that it spills over into depression and ill health. Certainly there's nothing wrong with seeking out practical steps for reducing everyday stress. Some of these techniques work quite well and are effective in producing a measure of peace temporarily.

God's Word teaches us, that as believers, we aren't to live as the world lives or to seek after man's methods. True and lasting peace comes only from God as it's a fruit of the Spirit.

The *calm* that God offers, and that I'm speaking about in this chapter, is altogether different; it's the pervasive, "all is well" kind of tranquility that enters a believer's soul. It's a calm that doesn't go away at the first sign of escalating difficulties or looming deadlines.

- "If a ruler's anger rises against you, do not leave your post; calmness can lay great errors to rest." (Ecclesiastes 10:4)
- "If your boss is angry at you, don't quit! A quiet spirit can overcome even great mistakes." (Ecclesiastes 10:4, NLT)

The fruit of the Spirit.

This calm comes from a source wholly different from the relative composure you can find in psychology. This calm comes from your Creator and it's a gift.

So how do we go about obtaining and benefiting from this invaluable blessing?

- "But the *fruit of the Spirit* is: **love, joy, peace, long-suffering, kindness, goodness, faithfulness, gentleness, self-control.**" (Galatians 5:22)

These nine attributes or gifts are from the Holy Spirit. Secular methods attempt to teach us how to exercise a measure of control over negative factors affecting us. But the Bible tells us that "*the fruit of the Sprit*" is **given** to us so we may experience joy and peace. They are the outcome of having the Holy Spirit and His work in our lives through salvation. Peace is evidence that a Christian has the Holy Spirit and is bearing "good fruit."

The Holy Spirit instills the *fruit of the Spirit* within us so we can operate at maximum efficiency, as we can't produce them in any long-term, consistent manner on our own. This means that God's love, joy, peace, gentleness, and kindness can be communicated into our being. His divine attributes are transferable to us when we accept Jesus Christ as our Savior. The Holy Spirit implants them within our heart at the time of our salvation, permanently transforming our inner being.

Think about the ramifications. God Himself allows us to share in His divine nature by imparting through His Holy Spirit, these divine qualities into our being and personality. This is why God specifically tells us in this verse that the "fruit" comes directly from His Spirit.

How can we begin to fully appreciate the magnitude of this transfer/transformation?

The word *"fruit"* in the Bible means something that "reproduces or shows profitability and usefulness." Jesus has already told us that He is the vine and we the branches. The branches draw their life from the vine. In the same way we draw our life directly from Jesus, who releases His life into us through the power of the Holy Spirit. He does this in the same way the tree releases life into its branches. Jesus is always our true vine from whom we draw strength.

In this short, but power-packed Scripture verse, God is giving us an incredible revelation of what goes on behind the scenes in the spiritual realm. The Holy Spirit makes possible our ability to love God, ourselves, and others. Peace, strength, and gentleness are just three examples of the divine attributes the Spirit imparts to us once we're in Christ.

These gifts allow us to live beyond what we see in this present, turbulent world. We can live with hope, knowing that God not only knows, but also controls all things. This assurance affords us immeasurable comfort, rest, and peace.

What are gentleness and strength?

Gentle doesn't mean mousy or weak. Gentleness in the New Testament sense means: strength derived from and under the control of the Holy Spirit.

All too frequently our natural response to others is harsh or at least impatient. As we grow weary, exasperated, and worn from life's seemingly endless demands, it's easy to lash out at others. Unfortunately, we're often the harshest with our own family and others who are closest to us. How sad that we so easily treat those who love us with such thoughtless scorn. Unless our natural tendencies are transformed by the power of the Holy Spirit, who goes to work on our carnal nature, we might not be able to genuinely love or even show kindness to others.

But a gentle woman will permit herself to take on the righteousness of Christ and be filled with the Holy Spirit to such a degree that she'll be known for her strength and gentleness.

God's glory shines forth from us when we permit Him to change our carnal nature and its tendencies. God desires the hidden person of our heart to be submitted to and ruled by Him. Only then can we develop a gentle and quiet spirit.

Responding to others with grace and strength is the *fruit* of a transformed life. When we grow closer to the Lord, He increases our gentleness. He quiets our soul when we hand Him our burdens and let Him fight our battles. We can experience greater peace knowing we have an omnipotent and altogether loving God on our side. He's willing to go before us and fight on our behalf.

God is the Giver of true peace and rest, and both become ours when we trust Him with all the events of our lives. The formula is easy, even if the process is not. Give up control—and gain rest. Constantly fighting battles is exhausting and leaves us vulnerable to defeat. Giving God our battles produces that gentle and quiet spirit within us.

Quiet doesn't mean silent, voiceless, or devoid of opinion. What it does mean comes closer to the literal, *without noise*. Quietness comes when we shut out the clamor created by too many voices incessantly competing to be heard. These voices want to introduce doubt, fear, and worry into our heart. When these conditions are present, there can be no peace. Be aware that difficult situations turn up the volume, making it extremely difficult to single out the voice of Jesus. Yet peace prevails when we're quieted before Him. From that peaceful place, the words of our mouth will be fitting, life-giving, and pleasing to God.

We prosper when God gives us clues to what pleases Him. He tells us that a gentle and quiet spirit is pleasing to Him. Any time God makes clear to us what He wants and how He operates, the information is of immense benefit to us.

Many want to justify responding to God with an annoyed, frustrated, or thankless attitude just because life at times, gets difficult. If you find yourself in an unbearable place, ask God for His wisdom in finding a workable solution, rather than merely complaining to Him about the situation. Ask Him to show you a way out, or a way to make peace with the difficulty.

If you're a quiet person by nature, don't presume that this is the quietness of God. Sometimes people are quiet because they're fearful, lacking the confidence to speak up. Or they may be preoccupied with their own welfare, not wanting to risk rejection from others. Such quietness is usually self-protective in nature.

God desire us to speak forth our testimony for Him. He wants His children to be positive and verbal examples of His work. Truth is He loves showing us off. God is the giver of "godly boldness" and He tells us to put our light on a table for all to see, not under a basket that will hide the rays of His reflected glory.

The apostle Peter emphasizes two realities about the Christian spirit: it is *meek* and it is *quiet*. He isn't addressing personality or temperament. Paul is speaking here of an ability, an attribute given by God. A meek and quiet spirit may be found in a woman who has a bubbly, outgoing, and vivacious personality.

What's beautiful to God?

Somewhere in our relationship with the Lord is a beautiful place called *divine deliverance*. Jesus released us from certain death through His redemptive work on the cross. Salvation is the first step in this process, when we choose to accept what He died to give us. Eventually, as we continue to push into Him, we sense our emancipation from our past and the things Satan used to hold us captive.

As our new being emerges, we become less harsh. As negative traits fall away from us, what's left is something beautiful, a radiant, glowing soul unencumbered and free to appropriate and appreciate intimacy with God.

When not to be silent.

In the coming difficult times, we must learn to speak out boldly for Christ. We can't afford to be self-conscience or inhibited. We aren't being motivated by the Spirit when we know someone is going in the wrong direction but won't share the "good news" with them.

Gentleness and restraint aren't an effective method in the face of dreadful or imminent peril, or even pervasive temptation that requires particular strength to fight against. We must teach people what's really working against them and keeping them from finding peace and truth.

When we're motivated by love in sharing the truth of God with others, God will show us how to do it effectively. He will, through prayer, speak to each of us uniquely.

God's definition of beauty.

Ask God to show you how and where you need to grow in gentleness and quietness. God loves it when we care about cultivating a spirit that pleases Him—a spirit that is quieted by His tenderness to us and offered in gentleness to others.

God's Word emphasizes that beauty can be found only in the work of Christ in the *heart*. Specifically in terms of a Christian woman, beauty isn't found at a cosmetic counter or even in following the latest fashion trends. It isn't in trying to replicate what we see in glamour and fashion magazines.

In contrast, the standard for a Christian woman is achieved in seeking after what God tells her is beautiful in His sight. Certainly we want to be tastefully fashionable and attractive. We hardly present a positive example of Christian womanhood if we are plain, dowdy, or dumpy. Being tasteful is being balanced.

Our femininity is a gift from God and it's to be highly regarded. Beautiful in God's sight is a woman whose heart and countenance longs for His approval. His beauty shines forth through her eyes, the windows into her soul. His loving gaze penetrates deep inside us, and He knows whether we desire to love Him wholeheartedly in return. The only great Lover of our soul, He cherishes everything about us and wants to hold first place in our heart.

Peter describes the kind of beauty God seeks. Beauty found in our *inner heart*, in that place Christ alone enters by grace to embed His life and exquisiteness within us.

- "Your beauty should not come from outward adornment, such as elaborate hairstyles and the wearing of gold jewelry or fine clothes. Rather, it should be that of your inner self, the unfading beauty of a gentle and quiet spirit, which is of great worth in God's sight." (1 Peter 3:3–4)

When our heart craves that which God longs for, we become one with Him. Our new person no longer looks for continuous attention from outside sources. God will give us all the attention we crave if we'll seek Him first. When we give Him first place in our love life, He lets us know we are beautiful to Him.

A child of God doesn't need to ask God to notice them, He already does! This brings us such confidence that we lose the desire to dress ourselves for attention. The Christian woman who embraces this truth radiates a beauty others recognize as rare and exceptional. It puts a glow on her face no amount of make-up can rival. The glory of God clothes us in His beauty and becomes our own.

Our spirit reflects our inward life as we live it out toward God. When the Holy Spirit enters a woman, her countenance and demeanor are changed. The existing nature of the child of God is different from what it was before.

How do we become meek and gentle in spirit?

A meek or gentle spirit doesn't insist on its own way. It isn't pushy, assertive, or demanding.

Scripture tells us that Moses was the humblest of men. Does that mean he wasn't a strong leader? Not at all! But Moses' strength didn't manifest itself through pushing his own agenda. He didn't consider himself to be self-important simply because God had chosen him to lead. He was well aware of his weaknesses and knew he wasn't a natural-born speaker. He didn't look at his leadership in terms of himself or his own ambitions.

God enjoys selecting those who aren't well equipped on their own to do what He asks of them. He's interested in the person who will remain humble and has to continuously look to Him to get the job done.

God alone wanted the glory for bringing His people out of captivity. He knew Moses, a meek and gentle man who followed the will of God, wouldn't try to usurp it for himself.

Meekness is the willing surrender by the grace of God of our own rights and advancement, along with a readiness to serve the advancement of God in others. The word "*quiet*" when used in this spiritual sense, is similar.

- "Make it your ambition to lead a quiet life: You should mind your own business and work with your hands, just as we told you." (1 Thessalonians 4:11)

Quietness in this sense is the absence of a turbulent, agitated spirit that manifests itself in being vulgar, aggressive, easily enraged, or overly loud. A meek and quiet spirit is one that embraces the will of God through subjecting oneself to His will. Meekness and quietness aren't graces appropriate only for women. They're Christian graces, based on inward strength and contentment.

We experience true peace and security when we bask in the Lord's leading, protection, acceptance, and love. The apostle Peter tells us that the impressive price of this beauty is found in two of its aspects.

1. *It isn't a corruptible beauty.*

Peter tells us that we have an inheritance that's incorruptible, undefiled, and that won't fade away.

> "Praise be to the God and Father of our Lord Jesus Christ! In his great mercy he has given us new birth into a living hope through the resurrection of Jesus Christ from the dead, and into *an inheritance that can never perish, spoil or fade.* This inheritance is kept in heaven for you, who through faith are shielded by God's power until the coming of the salvation that is ready to be revealed in the last time. In all this you greatly rejoice, though now for a little while you may have had to suffer grief in all kinds of trials. These have come so that the proven genuineness of your faith—*of greater worth than gold*, which perishes even though refined by fire—may result in praise, glory and honor when Jesus Christ is revealed. Though you have not seen him, you love him; and even though you do not see him now, you believe in him and are filled with an inexpressible and glorious joy, for you are receiving the end result of your faith, the salvation of your souls." (1 Peter 1:3–12)

> - "For you know that it was not with perishable things such as silver or gold that you were redeemed from the empty way of life handed down to you from your forefathers." (1 Peter 1:18)

We're redeemed by an incorruptible seed, which is Jesus. No one else can make that claim!

> - "For you have been born again, not of perishable seed, but of imperishable, through the living and enduring word of God." (1 Peter 1:23)

The beauty God gives to a Christian woman can't fade, grow lackluster with time, or perish. It's a beauty that lasts and doesn't grow old. In fact, this beauty mellows gracefully, becoming more beautiful with time, because the longer we walk with the Lord and learn to die to our self, the more appealing we become to others. Beautiful women of God are often those who are advanced in age. The laugh lines that accompany an authentic smile are attractive indeed.

2. *It's an imperishable, lasting, beauty.*

This beauty is costly because Jesus paid the ultimate price to give it to you. We owe it to Him to place great value to what He so highly cherishes—His Father's good pleasure. Our beauty as believing women is found in Christ Jesus alone. It's His life in you that makes you eternally and pricelessly beautiful.

Listen to the description by the Gospel writer Mark of the perfume Mary used to anoint Jesus:

- "While he was in Bethany, reclining at the table in the home of a man known as Simon the Leper, a woman came with an alabaster jar of very expensive perfume, made of pure nard. She broke the jar and poured the perfume on his head." (Mark 14:3)

When God sees us He sees His Son's beauty reflected in our faces. He sees in us a renewed heart fashioned by His own hands, a heart that wants to lavishly praise and please Him beyond measure.[1]

Is pleasing God important to you?

Every child of God wants His smile and dreads His displeasure. This "fear of the Lord" is beautiful to God.

Just as God can see your beauty, so a godly man will see the face of Christ shining through your inner, transformed beauty. If you're still single and the man you're dating doesn't see your beauty, it may be that he lacks the capacity to recognize great worth and value when he encounters it. If you're involved with someone who doesn't hold you in high esteem, consider being satisfied with God as your closest companion. He will guide your life to those who appreciate your true worth and beauty. Let Jesus fill your cup to overflowing. He alone will give you what you're looking for: gentleness, understanding, unconditional love, acceptance, and intimacy that isn't grasping for anything in return.

Be careful not to buy into the world's shallow ideas of companionship and beauty. Seek moderation in your approach to relationships. Authentic beauty is God's glory shining out of us. It's being conformed in word, thought, action, desires, and attitudes to Jesus Christ.

- "Like a gold ring in a pig's snout is a beautiful woman who shows no discretion." (Proverbs 11:22)

How you can become gentle and peaceful?

Invest in relationships with people who are godly, gentle, and peaceful. Surround yourself with those who possess the joy of the Lord, and before you know it you'll exhibit the same traits they're modeling. If you see something in another that you want, ask the person how they got to that place. But remember that the Holy Spirit is your greatest teacher and mentor. If you ask Him to teach you how to become gentle and joyful, He'll be delighted to comply.

Be sure to spend time in God's Word and in reading good Christian books. This will encourage you and lift you up from your current circumstances.

Avoid agitated, hateful people whose negative emotions will no doubt affect you in time. Build up your emotional account through kind words and actions directed toward others. Be careful and gracious with critique and let people know you appreciate them and what they do for you.

Be mindful of what brings you worry and stress.

God didn't create us for continual stress and fear. Giving in to these temptations only produces negative emotions that are detrimental to our overall well-being and health. Worry, if left unchecked, leads to anxiety, depression, and ultimately to uncontrollable fear. Over and over again in God's Word we're enjoined to "fear not and trust Him."

John tells us that we can have peace in this chaotic world, a peace available only "in" Him. If we want to overcome those incapacitating emotions, we must seek after the Giver of peace. Once we make it our priority to abide in Him, He'll take care of our provision and give us His peace.

- "I have told you these things, so that in me you may have peace. In this world you will have trouble. But take heart! I have overcome the world." (John 16:33)

John tells it like it is: We will have trouble in this world. It's a fact of the Christian life. All people experience trials, temptations, and suffering as a consequence of living in a fallen world. But Christians especially suffer because they're Christians. Yes, we can expect troubles, but we're empowered by the Holy Spirit to master those trials, not to be defeated by them.

There's a secret to conquering, to emerging not only unscathed, but victorious. Asking for and receiving wisdom is fundamental to knowing "the way out" of a situation. The Holy Spirit gives us revelation, eye-opening knowledge we need in order to know how and in what direction to go when we're overcome by circumstances. We may suffer "for a while" during hardship, but God commands us to take hold of our Christian authority to rebuke and defeat the devil.

Asking God to show us the way, and then trusting Him to provide for us in the midst of our difficulty, moves us into maturity in our relationship with Him. This process teaches us how to depend on and trust in Him with the events of our life. We must learn to believe God when He says He'll take care of us, otherwise unbelief will seep in and cause us to continually strive.

- "Cease striving and know that I am God." (Psalm 46:10, NAS).

God created us to enjoy us!

God is the initiator of relationship and fellowship, and we enjoy relationship with Him because He willed it.

God spent time *daily* with Adam and Eve in the Garden. This brought God enjoyment as man was created for His *good pleasure*. God was intentional in man's creation and He provided for him before He placed him in the garden. The garden was a peaceful, protected environment. God provided for Adam and Eve's every need, including food, shelter, companionship, and fellowship with Himself. They didn't need clothing because they were already clothed in His glory, and what's more, they had purposeful and fulfilling work to do.

If we believe we're on our own with no one to care for us, no one to help us in our time of need, we become overly burdened with the cares of this world and eventually become defeated and sick.

Striving is the world's way, not God's way! God always has the better way, but we must choose to believe Him to reap its effect in our life—*tranquility in the midst of turmoil.*

It's humbling to recognize that God's children have a direct line of communication with their heavenly Father. We don't respond to life as the world does because unbelievers don't know Him in the same personal way.

Take advantage of knowing the One who knows all things, including all our outcomes. Go to Him for advice and help in working out your situation. God is never preoccupied. He's ready and waiting at all times for you to pour out your soul to Him. Be sure to ask for His wisdom, which He promises to give liberally to those who do so (James 1:5).

God wants us to reach full maturity. If we're bringing problems on ourselves based on faulty beliefs and actions, we must ask God to move us away from these stumbling blocks. If we respond to His correction wrongly, He'll make clear to us that our beliefs and actions are moving us away from His purpose for us, not toward it.

Hardship doesn't form our character but reveals it.

Do you respond in anger when things don't go your way? When you get frustrated, do you act impulsively and make poor decisions as a result?

Reacting, as opposed to *responding*, is an emotional response. Instead, by letting God build your character into Christ-likeness you can rest in the quiet confidence that the Holy Spirit is already interceding on your behalf before the Father.

Refrain from getting caught up in emotion and drama. The Christian operates in a different way. Troubles won't vanish overnight, so while in the midst of a storm wait quietly and patiently for God to guide you through it. Only by relying on Him completely and learning to trust Him regardless of what the situation looks like, can you experience tranquility.

- "For everyone born of God overcomes the world. This is the victory that has overcome the world, even our faith" (1 John 5:3-5)

Learning to be still.

Until we learn to stop striving, especially during trying times, we'll be tempted to manipulate our circumstances. If we want God to work on our behalf, we need to rest on the promise that God has overcome the world. This is adding action to our understanding of the above verse. If you understand a verse and don't act upon that comprehension, you aren't letting go—and letting God!

While we often don't appreciate why we must go through trials, there's an underlying purpose for our hardships. God isn't arbitrary, nor does He send us hard times to teach us a lesson, as some believe. God isn't angry with us—He loves us. For some this concept will be difficult because everything they've been taught about God centers around His wrath.

The fact is that God long ago sent His son Jesus to take that righteous wrath upon Himself. But God will *allow* (not cause) the natural consequences of our own actions that aren't in line with His greater plans, to take their natural course to bring about better things in our lives.

Human parents understand the need for regular discipline of their children for the purpose of bringing about maturity. Their purpose is to better control undisciplined or negative behavior, and to move them toward positive behavior and attitudes. They do this so the child has a better outcome. This is discipline borne out of love.

Only selfish parents withhold discipline, taking the way of comfort and least resistance. But they're expressing a focus on themselves, not the well-being of the child. When we treat our children as our friends and confidants, without stepping in to guide, discipline, and direct them into maturity, we're being selfish and immature.

Compassion and empathy for others aren't a natural bent of children. All good character traits, including thinking of others more highly than oneself, must be cultivated. Adults notice when a young child is exhibiting these traits. They recognize that hard work and diligence on the part of the parents has produced such results.

If we as mothers in the natural realm understand this, wouldn't an all-loving, all-gracious God want to discipline us so that we might attain all the good things He has in store for us?

Discipline on the Father's part is to direct us to a different course. It only becomes a difficult path if we're rebellious toward God's intended redirection. If we're open and available to where He wants us to go, the discipline won't need to be longer, or more difficult, than necessary. We, not God, are often the ones who determine how long, and how stringent, the process must be.

We respond in the same way with our children. When "a look" is all it takes to chastise a little one, the process is virtually painless for both parties. But if the child is defiant and refuses to respond to our correction, we need to step it up a degree.

God is purposeful, never haphazard, in everything He does and permits. Our hardships serve His purposes, and although He doesn't directly bring them about, they have the potential to become positive experiences for us. That doesn't mean that everything will work according to *our* plans. But if we respond appropriately we may someday look back on those difficulties and recognize they were a catalyst to our spiritual growth.

An easy, problem-free life isn't conducive to the development of maturity or character. Quite the opposite! God, on the basis of His vast love for us, won't let us remain babes. That wouldn't be for our good.

A good parent makes a way for maturity to come about, and God is an excellent parent to us. He knows what we need even when we haven't got a clue. When we learn to stop questioning Him and His motives, we've learned to be still and trust Him.

The fruit of being still.

God rooted in us a yearning for His presence because He desired intimacy with each of us. That's the purpose for that void, that empty place in each of us. It can't be filled by any other person or means. It's both a God purposed and a God satisfied yearning.

But when we misread that longing and try to fill it with a God substitute, we find ourselves terribly disappointed. While work, hobbies, family, and friends are all enjoyable parts of our everyday life, if we aren't aware and careful, they'll become substitutes for the real thing—intimacy with Jesus. Only Christ's presence in our life can completely satisfy.

Worldly pursuits consume a lot of our valuable time. Time that could be spent giving Jesus the place He desires and deserves in our life. Work, interruptions, and excessive busyness, may distract us for awhile, but they'll never fill or satisfy us, as they were never meant to.

For believers, that inner void is filled by the presence of the Holy Spirit who takes up residence within us. Settle for no substitute. Seek until you find that which you've been engineered to crave.

You can be still and find rest only when you stop searching in all the wrong places for all the wrong people or things, when you accept the one right solution, Jesus Christ. He's the prize, the treasure, and the reward for remaining still long enough to recognize that nothing else will satisfy.

He made you that way for a reason—*so He could have you.* His presence empowers you to live with joy, peace, and rest. He gives you the ability to stop striving and to wholly enjoy Him, when you're quiet and amenable to receiving from Him.

All good fathers provide for their children. But He's the only *perfect* Father, the only One who'll never let you down. God takes care of what belongs to Him, and that includes you.

- "I will never leave you nor forsake you." (Hebrews 13:5)
- "God is not human, that he should lie, not a human being, that he should change his mind. Does he speak and then not act? Does he promise and not fulfill? (Numbers 23:19)

Quiet reverence will allow God to reveal Himself to you.

If you've never truly experienced the presence of God, you may wonder how He reveals Himself to believers. The Lord has many different ways of reaching out to His children and making Himself known. There are many ways in which God communicates with His children:

1. ***God speaks***—You may never hear God's audible voice, but He'll speak to your heart just the same. His "voice" is so unmistakable that those who hear and listen to Him remember long after the fact

both the message and the excitement of His choosing to speak to them.

2. *God sends a message*—Sometimes God lays a compulsion upon a person's heart to spend time with Him. They may sense a desire to block out the world for a time to be alone with Him. He often sends His children messages through prayer or the reading of His Word. Or, it may come when we're quietly listening to a spoken message, whether in church, on Christian TV, or radio program. If we don't give Him this opportunity by finding a time and place to be quiet and alone, open and even actively listening for Him to speak, we may not hear. It's unwise to ignore such urgings. Don't make the mistake of waiting for a more convenient time. God's timing is always impeccable, and it will be harder to hear Him later if you put Him off. There's nothing more humbling and awesome than when God chooses to speak to us. We show Him the love and respect that are due Him when we gladly rearrange our schedule to show Him how important He is to us. Choose to reverence and cherish this very special relationship God is initiating with you. You're life will never again be the same when this becomes your all-out priority in life.

   - "I will praise the Lord, who counsels me; even at night my heart instructs me. I have set the Lord always before me. Because he is at my right hand, I will not be shaken. Therefore my heart is glad and my tongue rejoices; my body also will rest secure." (Psalm 16:7–9)

3. *God makes His presence known through His Word*—God will give us the answers we're looking for when we read His Word. Be careful not to demand always hearing from Him by your chosen method. He left you His Word, and it's one of His primary methods of speaking to you. If we're prone to thinking that God doesn't communicate with us, it may be that we haven't gone to the Word with the expectation of hearing His voice.

4. *God makes His presence known through His people*—Sometimes God speaks through one of His servants. Someone with the spiritual gift of prophecy, wisdom, or a "word of knowledge" can often cut through the chaos of events and clarify both the problem and the

solution for us. Learn to appreciate mature Christians who may hold the word we need.

Repentance bears "good fruit."

True repentance will bear fruit. Conflict frequently makes us want to rush in and defend ourselves, to justify our behavior and position. But James gives us different advice:

- "My dear brothers and sisters, take note of this: Everyone should be quick to listen, slow to speak and slow to become angry." (James 1:19)

So much more can be accomplished with a calm, unruffled approach as the Scriptures indicate.

1. *Pray*—Ask the Lord for the wisdom to guard your tongue. Ask Him to make you a peacemaker, not a troublemaker.

2. *See through God's eyes*—God has a divine perspective on every-thing He does in a believer's life. He's working in all things for our long-term, ultimate benefit (Romans 8:28). We show the world our transformed lives when we respond appropriately.

3. *Forgive*—Even when someone has hurt us or caused us humiliation and pain, God requires that we forgive, just as He has so graciously forgiven us. Jesus died so we could be forgiven of all our sins— past, present, and future. And as forgiven sinners, we have no right to withhold forgiveness from others. Forgiving others benefits both them and our selves. When we forgive, we experience freedom from bitterness, hardness of heart, resentment, broken relationships, ill health, and preoccupation with revenge.

   In contrast, we're kept in bondage when we refuse to forgive. It isn't our prerogative to defiantly disobey a direct command from God. We're never to choose attitudes and behaviors that put ourselves above Him.

4. *Respond*—At the other end of the spectrum, when we've wronged others we're to apologize and ask them to forgive us. When someone lets us know that we've offended them, whether or not we were aware of the situation, we owe it both to them and to God to be quick to apologize. Thank them for the willingness to share their feelings with us, assuring them that we'll carefully consider their

comments. Even if we disagree with their assessment of a situation, there's no harm in saying we'll consider their argument or viewpoint. Nor can apologizing hurt the relationship. Giving up our "right to be right" is something many of us with strong personalities find particularly difficult. This attitude requires dying to self. If we're willing to relinquish our perceived "rights," we might be surprised at the results. For one thing, our pride won't have an opportunity to get the best of us. Pride can be so insidious, in fact, it's one of Satan's best weapons, because it entices us to hold grudges against God, not just others. If we break off our relationship with the Lord, we have no other mediator or recourse. We're in continuous need of Christ's mediation for us through His Spirit. Without it, Satan will quickly and efficiently snatch us away.[2]

- "For there is one God and one mediator between God and mankind, the man Christ Jesus, who gave himself as a ransom for all people. This has now been witnessed to at the proper time." (1 Timothy 2:5–6)

The power of grace is for everyone.

It's God's desire for every person to *know* Him personally—not just know about Him. That God desires this level of intimacy with us is the most telling aspect of His character. For many, God seems far away and highly impersonal, but when we search the Scriptures accurately, we know this isn't true.

- David asked of God, "What is man that you are mindful of him, the son of man that you care for him?" (Psalm 8:4)
- And Paul in 1 Timothy 2:4 tells us that God "desires all men to be saved and to come to the knowledge of the truth."

Notice that Paul doesn't say that God wanted only some, perhaps just a select few, to know the truth. No, He wants everyone on earth to be saved and to be in relationship with Him.

God knows that each individual must accept and receive the salvation He offers to spend eternity with Him. He gave up His Son, Jesus for us. This is His chosen method of liberating us.

Repentance leads to salvation and it's a good thing, as it affords us life. Repentance brings us to God, and since God is life, repentance brings us to life—life eternal, at that.

- Rather, "The Lord is not slow in keeping his promise, as some understand slowness. He is patient with you, not wanting anyone to perish, but everyone to come to repentance." (2 Peter 3:9)

Unbelievers sometimes think their sins are too great for God to forgive. But the moment we're willing to acknowledge and confess our wrongdoing, the Lord accepts us as His child, no strings attached.

God is in the "cleanup" business. He isn't dependent on our presenting ourselves as clean before He'll "take" us. That's Satan's lie to keep us from approaching God just as we are. God will joyfully accept all who come to Him in true repentance. And that includes the dirty, impure, prideful, or habitually deceived. Those impurities are a result of sin, and we're all alike, sinners in need of a Savior.

Incredibly, when we present ourselves to Him, He sees us, not our sin. He took care of the sin "problem" a long time ago with Jesus' death on the cross. Regardless of what we may have done to dishonor Him, God is standing by, ready and willing to forgive and incorporate us into His family. When we make the choice of belonging to Him we inherit the *whole* kingdom of God.

It's humbling, even for those of us who've been Christians for a long time, to reflect on God's goodness, demonstrated particularly in His free gift of salvation.

When our hearts have grown cold toward His love and goodness, we can still move forward by asking Him to forgive us. Humbling ourselves softens our calloused hearts and builds intimate fellowship once again. We can be safe in the knowledge that no mistake can ever put us beyond the reach of His love.

Ask according to His will.

We're all seeking something, and when we become God's child that doesn't change, because people are born with many needs. Initially in our relationship with God we tend to ask Him for *things*. But John clarifies what it is God promises to grant.

- "Now this is the confidence that we have in Him, that if we ask anything *according to His will*, He hears us." (1 John 5:14)

Real prayer is communion, being like-minded with God. Although salvation comes the moment we ask Christ into our heart, the sanctification process occurs over time. In due course, we learn what it means to ask in His will.

The word *sanctify* originates from the Greek *hagiazo*, which means to separate or set apart. Sanctification relates to a sovereign act of God whereby He "sets apart" a person, place, or thing to accomplish His purpose. Sanctification, an act of the Spirit, is the process by which the believer becomes more and more conformed to Christ's image and likeness. We take on Christ's desires and vision for our lives as we take on His heart. Our desires are no longer carnal in nature once we invite the sanctification process to take place in us.

We're less likely to ask wrongly once we've been transformed by the Holy Spirit and know more of God's will. In fact, He fills our mind and heart with His own thoughts when we submit to Him. His desires become our desires when we pray and ask according to His will.

- "When you ask, you do not receive, because you ask with wrong motives, that you may spend what you get on your pleasures." (James 4:3)

We must come away with the realization that prayer isn't dictating to God. It's a humble, heartfelt expression of our dependency upon Him. The one who prays rightly is submissive to God's will.

A gentle and peaceful countenance is beautiful to the Lord.

Our heart's desire must be to please and obey God. But our flesh and willpower are weak making sin difficult to resist. Yet, it's within the context of our continual struggle with sin and our seeking to obey God that sanctification does its mightiest work. It's the inward work of the Holy Spirit which brings about our holiness and change.

We begin to view the world, people, and personal difficulties from a different standpoint—from a more biblical perspective. Our choices begin to be motivated by love, truth, and holiness.

In the past we may have misplaced our confidence and security, seeking after worldly beauty, wealth, and covetousness. But when our heart is turned away from the world and toward God, we become liberated from such growth-hindering snares. The transformation process may be painful, but it's always motivated by God's love for us.

Decide today to let the Holy Spirit go to work on your behalf and turn you into someone beautiful to behold—someone with a gentle and peaceful countenance. It'll be your best witness to the angry world around you.

5

SHE KNOWS THAT PRAYER AND FAITH ARE THE REMEDY FOR FEAR

"For God has not given us a spirit of fear, but of power and of love and of a sound mind." (2 Timothy 1:7) "Have I not commanded you? Be strong and courageous. Do not be terrified, do not be discouraged, for the Lord your God will be with you wherever you go." (Joshua 1:9)

Fear is toxic and lethal and it will kill us unless we know the cure. Fear is more than an emotion—it's a spirit! A spirit, that if not controlled, will undermine our very faith and future.

Fear is Satan's preferred strategy against us because it works so well. It's effective because it keeps us from discovering God's true love and power to transform us. When we succumb to this one efficient weapon in the devil's arsenal, we become paralyzed.

Faith is both the opposite of fear and its failsafe remedy. And its prayer that makes faith operational in our lives.

- "For God has not given us a spirit of fear, but of power and of love and of a sound mind." (2 Timothy 1:7).

Paul made this declaration to his younger protégé Timothy, telling him at the same time to stir up his spiritual gifts, testify for Jesus Christ, and share with Paul in suffering for the gospel of Jesus Christ. In essence, Paul was telling Timothy that he was responsible for stirring up his own gifts.

God has already given us everything we need to stay strong in His power. The Holy Spirit makes this possible. When we stay in His presence through prayer, praise, and worship—we build ourselves up in our faith.

Many continually ask God to stir them up, but they're praying wrongly, and they won't see the answers they seek. Rather, we need to know what the Holy Spirit has already given us. He alone makes us strong, confident, and powerful. He gives us the necessary wisdom to defeat Satan and to remain strong in our faith. Scripture tells us that we're fully equipped, lacking nothing (Colossians 2:9–10).

Satan doesn't want you to use your spiritual gifts, talk to others about Jesus, or be joyful and free from fear. He wants you to believe that if you speak up for Jesus you'll be persecuted and ridiculed. We must carry within us the genuine knowledge of God to be delivered from this evil spirit.

Fear not only prevents God's people from witnessing and effectively using their gifts, but it stops them from finding "delight in the Lord." This is the joy to which Christians are called. We belong to the One who gave it to us as our rightful inheritance.

The fear of rejection has hindered people from coming to God. They fear asking Him for forgiveness, beginning new relationships, launching a new business venture or ministry, or moving forward in an area to which God is calling them.

The fear of failure keeps multitudes from moving from ordinary to extraordinary. The fear of death paralyzes and torments throngs of people. There are many varieties of fear, but they all have something in common: fear of every type (except for the reverential "fear" we hold for God) comes from Satan.

Unfortunately, countless Christians have received, accepted, and allowed the spirit of fear, which is a curse, to enter their lives. In many cases this occurred before they became Christians. Many after becoming a Christian lack understanding that God's power can eradicate this devouring spirit.

- "Through knowledge the righteous will be delivered." (Proverbs 11:9)

Many pastors avoid preaching on this topic and seem to be unaware that fear is a spirit sent from Satan to control a person. A lack of understanding of how Satan works against us makes his job all the more effective. Countless people don't believe in demons or evil spirits. Yet they are often the ones suffering the most from the agonizing effects of anxiety and dread, and the torment they bring.

The real secret to ending all fear.

There are two distinct reasons people have difficulty finding peace and remaining in it:

1. They don't have a proper view or understanding of the character and governance of God.

2. When His true character is made known to them, they don't put their confidence in Him. They find no pleasure in receiving the truth about God.

Both of these difficulties must he removed before people can be reconciled to their Creator. Only when we bother to study God's true nature and character, do we see that He alone is our answer and deserves our complete confidence.

We often have faulty views of God because we're prone to human error. We mistakenly feel justified in "judging" God, His work, His methods of governing, and even His character. We're naturally arrogant and prideful and don't even recognize this tendency. We set ourselves up as judge and jury believing that we hold all truth. We believe we're the most reliable source of our confidence. We form our own religions rather than embrace "the way, the truth, and the life" God has revealed to us. We rely on our own works for salvation rather than stooping to accept God's "plan of salvation." And we refuse to acknowledge that He's the One who stooped from divinity to death on our behalf.

We don't hold all wisdom! In our ignorance and perplexity we don't bother to go to God and ask Him our questions about His being and doing. We don't confer with Him regarding our decisions, direction, purpose, or how to find true satisfaction with the life we've been handed.

People are prone to difficulties because they prefer to rely upon themselves. They refuse to humbly submit to someone who knows more than they do. Pride is the primary reason people remain in fear—despite Jesus having come to remedy the problem.

Many of us believe that our problems stem from others, but the root culprit is: *a lack of love for God.*

When people disbelieve God and His Word, they don't perceive Him as worthy to be the Sovereign Lord of the universe. Our world is an uncertain place, to put it mildly. We have no control over natural disasters, global financial downfalls, or that pervasive sense of impending doom as we draw closer to the end of the world as we know it. Without confidence in the Lord, we can have no confidence in life. There's one fact nobody can ignore: our end is certain.

How to rid yourself of fear.

No Christian receives a "spirit of fear" from God. To the contrary, fear comes from being *separated* from God. In fact, we learn in 1 John 4:18 that "perfect love casts out fear." God is the epitome and essence of that perfect love. Faith in God is the failsafe remedy to deliver us from the evil Satan so enjoys attaching to us.

- In the words of Jesus, "What do you mean, 'If I can'? Anything is possible if a person believes." (Mark 9:23, NLT)

Fear is the opposite of faith and faith is the antidote to fear. We can't live in fear and in faith at the same time. Fear must be confronted head-on with the power of faith. Fear paralyzes us and keeps us from receiving God's promises. It holds us back, preventing us from stepping out in obedience to what God has called us to do. It keeps us from our destiny and from living a full and productive life that blesses God, others, and ourselves.

We must proclaim the Word of God and *command fear to leave us.* This is taking action against our fear. Don't accept the fear or Satan's messages to you. If you're a believer, he isn't your father and you don't need to listen to him any longer. If you aren't a believer, you can become one by simply asking God to enter your life and change you within.

James tells us that when we find ourselves in need we should come to God in simple *belief* and ask Him for whatever it is we lack. That word is vitally important. By exercising continual, trusting faith, we can overcome fear.[1]

- "If any of you lacks wisdom, let him ask of God, who gives to all liberally and without reproach, and it will be given to him. But let him ask in faith, with no doubting, for he who doubts is like a wave of the sea driven and tossed by the wind. For let not that man suppose that he will receive anything from the Lord." (James 1:5–7)
- "Confess your trespasses to one another, and pray for one another, that you may be healed. The effective, fervent prayer of a righteous man avails much." (James 5:16)

The keys to heaven.

When we make confession with our mouth, we're releasing our faith. This is the *secret* to the kingdom of heaven.

- "And I will give you the keys of the kingdom of heaven, and whatever you bind on earth will be bound in heaven, and whatever you loose on earth will be loosed in heaven." (Matthew 16:19)

Confessing Scripture in prayer is important because it opens the doors of heaven to us. When we speak them outwardly, we establish or confirm the things we believe inwardly. When we do this, we're establishing in the spiritual realm the words we speak in the physical realm. With time, what's established spiritually will be manifested physically.

When we speak truths like, "*I believe in your Word, and that Word says that everything I put my hand to will prosper and succeed,*" we're agreeing with God.

God declared that He gave us a spirit not of fear but of *power,* of *love,* and of a *sound mind.* In response, we should be confessing continually "I will fear not!"

Scripture assures you that you do indeed have a sound mind, so confess (speak it forth) and believe it. (2 Timothy 1:7).

God expects us to build up our faith—a faith that's like a rock.

When we learn the proper methods and go to the right person, Jesus, to build up a rock-solid faith, Scripture tells us that hell itself is power-less against us.

- "Jesus answered and said to him, 'Blessed are you, Simon Bar-Jonah, for flesh and blood has not revealed this to you, but my father who is in heaven. And I also say to you that you are Peter, and on this rock I will build my church, and the gates of Hades shall not prevail against it.'" (Matthew 16:17–18)

Faith that is stable and completely reliant on the Lord affords us an unshakeable confidence. Faith lets us know to whom we belong, and nothing will change that fact. This is the confidence that comes from being a child of God, a confidence that's visible and unshakable, and is baffling to the world and those who don't know Him.

God gave Abraham a promise.

Abram (later Abraham) was called according to God's purposes.

- "The Lord had said to Abram, 'Leave your country, your people and your father's household and go to the land I will show you. I will make you into a great nation and I will bless you; I will make your name great, and you will be a blessing. I will bless those who bless you, and whoever curses you I will curse; and all peoples on earth will be blessed through you." (Genesis 12:1–3)

God's desire was that all nations be blessed, and He would accomplish this through Abraham's calling. Centuries later, when Paul spoke of God's purpose for Abraham, he explained that Scripture had foreseen that God would justify the Gentiles by faith and that God had announced the gospel in advance to Abraham.

- "All nations will be blessed through you." (Galatians 3:8)

God revealed His purpose even before Israel had been formed as a nation. God spoke to Abraham again, saying,

- "Lift up your eyes from where you are and look north and south, east and west. All the land that you see I will give to you and your offspring forever." (Genesis 13:14–15)

God had more in mind than blessing Abraham with land. His bigger picture was that Abraham, *on account of his faith*, would produce through his seed a new generation. Through Abraham's bloodline God would have a people of faith for Himself. God counted Abraham's faith "as righteousness," and through his seed a generation of righteous people would be produced.

God always has more in mind than we can begin to imagine. His vision for us is infinitely more discriminating than our own. He blesses us for faith and obedience, as they demonstrate to Him that we trust in His vision for us. When we see with God's perspective, fear fades, and we're able to carry out God's purposes and plan for our life. Our prayers present our praises and petitions before a God who has a purpose for our lives we don't yet see, at least not in its entirety. We bring our requests and needs before Him because we're confident He answers the prayers of His children.

Relationship matters! Just as earthly fathers love to have their children come to them with their concerns about life, our heavenly Father desires the same. Children are trying to grow up, to make their way through the maze of life's complexities. We're to do the same with Jesus. He helps us navigate life wisely making our steps sure and our foundation strong even in adversity.

There are five kinds of petitions that are always appropriate to bring before God, especially in times of fear or uncertainty: petitions for *forgiveness, protection, strength, direction,* and *purpose.* But it is praise that brings God's presence and power to bear in our lives. This includes the power of His healing.

- "Come to me, all you who are weary and burdened, and I will give you rest. Take my yoke upon you and learn from me, for I am gentle and humble in heart, and you will find rest for your souls. For my yoke is easy and my burden is light." (Matthew 11:28–30)

Paul reminds us how to handle fear,

- ***"Be strong in the Lord and in his mighty power. Put on the full armor of God so that you can take your stand against the devil's schemes.*** For our struggle is not against flesh and blood, but against the rulers, against the authorities, against the powers of this dark world and against the spiritual forces of evil in the heavenly realms. Therefore put on the full armor of God, so that when the day of evil comes, you may be able to stand your ground, and after you have done everything, to stand. Stand firm then, with the belt of truth buckled around your waist, with the breastplate of righteousness in place, and with your feet fitted with the readiness that comes from the gospel of peace. In addition to all this, take up the shield of faith, with which you can extinguish all the flaming arrows of the evil one. Take the helmet of salvation and the sword of the Spirit, which is the word of God. And pray in the Spirit on all occasions with all kinds of prayers and requests." (Ephesians 6:10–18)

Jesus condenses the Old Testament message to two verses in Luke.

- "He told them, 'This is what is written: The Christ will suffer and rise from the dead on the third day, and repentance and forgiveness of sins will be preached in his name to all nations, beginning at Jerusalem. This is what I told you while I was still with you: *Everything must be fulfilled that is written about me in the Law of Moses, the Prophets and the Psalms*.'" (Luke 24:46–47)

A seed would come, die, and be resurrected, and repentance and the forgiveness of sins in His name would be proclaimed to all nations. Jesus added,

- "And you are witnesses of these things." (Luke 24:48)

What a privilege for these humble men of God's choosing. Jesus reminded his disciples, however, not to rush out immediately to spread the good news. Instead He commanded:

- "I am going to send you what my Father has promised; but stay in the city until you have been clothed with *power from on high*." (Luke 24:49)

This is the same vision we must catch and the method we should follow: to refrain from going out under our own power, which would render the work either fruitless or nearly so, but to wait upon the Holy Spirit who empowers us for a mighty harvest.

This is God's purpose for every Christian. Until we understand that Satan will try and use the *spirit of fear* to deter our purpose, we may never come to see that purpose fulfilled. It is only through the spoken Word that we renounce this evil spirit. It is through the power of the Holy Spirit that we move into our destiny as strong, fruit-bearing Christians. With our faith strong, we like Abraham, produce a generation of righteous, not fearful, people.

Once we catch the overall message of the Bible, we see the reason for the baptism of the Holy Spirit—to anoint us for service and enable us to be bold witnesses for Christ. We see the reason for the gifts of the Holy Spirit—which empower us to serve God effectually by spreading the "good news" to the lost and to edify the body of Christ.

This is why Jesus instructs us on holy living. That our light might shine powerfully before others, that they may see our good works and glorify our Father in heaven. Paul put it this way:

- "But I have had God's help to this very day, and so I stand here and testify to small and great alike. I am saying nothing beyond what the prophets and Moses said would happen—that the Christ would suffer and, as the first to rise from the dead, would proclaim light to his own people and to the Gentiles." (Acts 26:22–23)

How King David controlled his fear.

Psalm 27 was crafted by David, who on numerous occasions experienced unyielding fear as his constant companion. While still a young shepherd boy David had fought off a lion and a bear and killed the giant Goliath. Much of his adult life was spent fighting wars. Before he was anointed king he spent years running from demented King Saul, who in jealousy was intent on killing him.

These experiences left David understanding the *spirit of fear*. His psalms comprise his intimate written accounts of his communion with God. With candid transparency he poured out his heart in weariness and at times in great fear and anguish to the Lord.

By the time the Holy Spirit inspired David to write Psalm 27, the psalmist was older and wiser. The passage of years had taught him a new way of relating to God. He had also learned how better to handle the problem of fear.

Instead of pleading with God, we see a man who is confident in His Lord. We see David's progression from *fearful* to *fearless*. He has matured. He has weathered many storms. He has learned a new way of communing with God. Now he speaks of what (or who) God is, and of his reasons for confidence in His Lord. David's countenance was changed when he learned to take a new approach—when he could speak faith, rather than fear.

What's the lesson for us here? Rather than speaking our fear, we're to speak of our confidence in God. He alone is mighty and completely trustworthy! This retrains our focus, moving it to where it should be, on the One who goes to battle for us. In the process it builds our faith and trust in Him, bringing glory to God as we speak forth our confidence.

As a side benefit, we enjoy our relationship with God more when our focus is on Him rather than on ourselves and our personal concerns. Life will always have its anxieties; for this reason the Scriptures speak so often on the topic of trusting God by giving our concerns over to Him.

Without this turn, we will be unable to enjoy the Lord or to bask in His love as He intended.[2]

David's psalm of fearless trust in God.

- "The Lord is my light and my salvation—whom shall I fear? The Lord is the stronghold of my life—of whom shall I be afraid? When evil men advance against me to devour my flesh, and when my enemies and my foes attack me, they will stumble and fall. Though an army besiege me, my heart will not fear; though war break out against me, even then will I be confident. One thing I ask of the Lord, this is what I seek: that I may dwell in the house of the Lord all the days of my life, to gaze upon the beauty of the Lord and to seek him in his temple. For in the day of trouble he will keep me safe in his dwelling; he will hide me in the shelter of his tabernacle and set me high upon a rock. Then my head will be exalted above the enemies who surround me; at his tabernacle will I sacrifice with shouts of joy; I will sing and make music to the Lord. Hear my voice when I call, O Lord; be merciful to me and answer me. My heart says of you "Seek his face!" Your face, Lord, I will seek. Do not hide your face from me, do not turn your servant away in anger; you have been my helper. Do not reject me or forsake me, O God my Savior. Though my father and mother forsake me, the Lord will receive me. Teach me your way, O Lord; lead me in a straight path because of my oppressors. Do not turn me over to the desire of my foes, for false witnesses rise up against me, breathing out violence. I am still confident of this: I will see the goodness of the Lord in the land of the living. Wait for the Lord; be strong and take heart and wait for the Lord." (Psalm 27)

David specifies four actions that will quiet our fear.

1. *"Faith" will quiet our fears.* (Psalm 27:1–3)

   Make God your *source:* "He's my light."

   Make God your *escape:* "He's my salvation."

   Make God your *security:* "He's my stronghold."

2. *"Worship" will quiet our fears*. (Psalm 27:4–6)

Worship God by your *lifestyle:* "Dwell in the house of the Lord."

Worship God by your *praise:* "Gaze upon the beauty of the Lord."

Worship God by your *priorities:* "Seek him in his temple."

Worship God by your *giving:* "Sacrifice with shouts of joy."

Worship God by your *singing:* "Sing and make music to the Lord."

3. *"Prayer" quiets our fears*. (Psalm 27:7–10)

Pray by *calling* on God.

Pray by *seeking* God.

4. *"Submission" quiets our fears*. (Proverbs 27:11–14)

Learning from God: "Teach me your way, O Lord."

Following God: "Lead me in a straight path."

Hoping in God: "Wait for the Lord."

Wandering the wilderness in unbelief produces fear and death.

God worked to free the older generation of Israelites from bondage in Egypt, yet despite their hardship and all the miracles they saw God perform on their behalf, they didn't enter the Promised Land. Instead, they circled around a mountain until they died off. Why did it take them forty years to accomplish what should have been an eleven-day trek? Although God had freed them from their slavery in Egypt, they *refused to see themselves as free.*

This is a major lesson for each of us. That generation didn't enter the Promised Land, not because it was impossible for them to do so, but on the basis of one problem: *they refused to overcome their "slave mentality."* In other words, they brought their slavery mindset with them into the desert, their passageway into a new future. This fresh start was to bring them out of slavery, but they chose to *remain* enslaved. They couldn't enter into the new, because they wouldn't leave behind the old.

The Israelites refused to change their thought patterns, and in consequence, their attitudes and conduct continued to reflect their lives while in captivity. Mind you, God showed them His majesty, His power,

79

and His attributes again and again and continually demonstrated His mercy to them. They saw God at work, working astounding miracles on their behalf. They witnessed the punishment the Egyptians experienced at God's hand. They saw how God parted the Red Sea and how He led them in the wilderness under a cloud by day and a pillar of fire by night. Never were they left alone by God, nor did He ignore their daily needs for shelter, nourishment, and water.

But for these "stiff-necked" unbelieving Israelites, the wilderness proved to be nothing more than a vast spiritual wasteland experience. They reaped barrenness for their *unbelief.* If they had simply been able to change their thinking and believe in their hearts what they witnessed God doing in their lives and circumstances, they could have experienced abundant blessing despite the inhospitable surroundings. Since they wouldn't keep the goal in their sights, the wilderness became the cemetery in which they wandered for all or most of forty years before eventually dying.

- "These things happened to them as examples and were written down as warnings for us, on whom the culmination of the ages has come." (1 Corinthians 10:11)
- "And who made God angry for forty years? Wasn't it the people who sinned, whose corpses lay in the wilderness?" (Hebrews 3:17, NLT)

The warning is clear for those of us living in the time in which many expect the Lord to return. This account represents a spiritual journey for each of us.

Canaan, the Promised Land, symbolized the kingdom of God. Hebrews 3:17, pictures a scattering of most likely unburied bodies. These corpses were the remains of the same people who had emerged from Egypt overjoyed at their new found liberty. They were finally to receive from the Lord what they had dreamed of for so many years—to be settled in their own land. But instead of freedom, they chose bondage.

They could have reached out for what God was so willing to give them—a land overflowing with blessing. But rather than reaching out *in faith* toward what God had for them, they returned to familiar beliefs, thinking, and behaviors that would lead them to impoverishment, landlessness, and bitterness. God showed them His care through miracles, yet in return they offered Him lack of character, lack of faith, and a stubborn refusal to turn from their natural bent toward sin and unbelief.

Paul verbalizes why their hearts seemingly couldn't be changed, why they consistently and persistently sinned and rebelled against the very Lord who had chosen them as His own. The apostle redirects this line of thought into an admonition for us.

- "So we see that because of their **unbelief** they were not able to enter his rest." (Hebrews 3:19)

We, like God's ancient people, are able to enter God's rest if we refuse to mix our belief with *unbelief*. The gospel, as Paul pointed out, was preached to *all*, not just to the Israelites. We profit by that Word when we show our faith in God.

- "God's promise of entering his rest still stands, so we ought to tremble with fear that some of you might fail to experience it. For this good news—that God has prepared this rest—has been announced to us just as it was to them. But it did them no good because they didn't share the faith of those who listened to God." (Hebrews 4:1–2)

God's grace keeps us from receiving what we justly deserve, no matter how hard some of us insist on going after it. But there comes a point at which God will give someone over to his or her own distortion of truth and continual unbelief. This unbelief in a good God, leads us in one direction: toward fear and death. We must not allow such a powerful lesson to pass by unheeded. Again in Paul's words:

- "Such things were written in the Scriptures long ago to teach us. And the Scriptures give us **hope** and **encouragement** as we wait patiently for God's promises to be fulfilled." (Romans 15:4)

The lesson is clear. Those who believe God must reveal and declare their faith by obeying Him. Those who don't believe, disobey. Hebrews 3:12 tells us that unbelief is evidence of an evil heart, and an evil heart can only depart from God.

- "Be careful then, dear brothers and sisters. Make sure that your own hearts are not evil and unbelieving, turning you away from the living God." (Hebrews 3:12)

- "And who was it who rebelled against God, even though they heard his voice? Wasn't it the people Moses led out of Egypt? (Hebrews 3:16; Hebrews 3:17–4:2)

How important is faith?

- "In just a little while, he who is coming will come and will not delay." And, "But my righteous one will live by faith. And *I take no pleasure in the one who shrinks back*." (Hebrews 10:37–38)
- "See, the enemy is puffed up; his desires are not upright—but the righteous person will live by his faithfulness." (Habakkuk 2:4)

That "the just will live by faith" (Hebrews 10:38) is both a statement and a fact. It speaks to the reality that this is how a Christian is to live, and God commands it of us. One definition of *faith* is complete trust, confidence, or reliance. *Belief* is listed as a synonym and it means faith (especially religious faith), trust, or confidence. These two words are virtually synonymous.

But the Bible differentiates between the two, making it clear that there's a qualitative difference between merely believing and *living by faith*, since believers are called to walk by faith and not by sight (2 Corinthians 5:7).

Many people acknowledge that God exists, but they don't trust Him with their lives. The practical application of faith is more than simply acknowledging the reality of God. Someone may believe "*in*" God (believe that He exists) but not "*believe*" God with their life, or agree to trust Him where the "rubber meets the road." When we hand ourselves over to God, believing that He can do something infinitely better with our lives than we can, we're revealing our trust is in Him. Living in faithfulness means: trusting Him with the results regardless what the situation may look like from our limited perspective.

When we determine to remain obedient when our every impulse is to flee in fear, faithfulness is the end product of our perseverance. When our determination and resolve are built up, we're less likely to be swept away by every ripple of life. We know how to respond to stress and uncertainty, for we've done it before, and have found our God faithful in all things.

The right kind of faith (Hebrews 11:1).

- "Now faith is *confidence* in what we hope for and *assurance* about what we do not see." (Hebrews 11:1, NIV)

- In the ESV, "Now faith is the *assurance* of things hoped for, the *conviction* of things not seen."

- And in the KJV, "Now faith is the *substance* of things hoped for, the *evidence* of things not seen."

- "Nevertheless, God's solid foundation stands firm, sealed with this inscription: 'The Lord knows those who are His,' and, 'Everyone who confesses the name of the Lord must turn away from wickedness'" (2 Timothy 2:19).

Paul is saying that *faith* is the Christian's foundation on which all else is built. All buildings must have a solid foundation, one that tunnels deep into the ground to keep it standing strong in the face of fierce weather. For the Christian, that which remains unseen by others, our deep, undergirding foundation, keeps us from wavering when the storms of life rear.

Oftentimes it isn't until a crisis occurs that others wonder at our calm demeanor, the outward manifestation of the substance, confidence, and assurance of our faith. When gale-force winds tear away the topsoil, the girders of our foundation stand exposed for all to see. We don't collapse in a heap of rubble when troubles come our way. We don't react with the dismay of the unbelieving world, nor do we fail to respond positively when we see God doing the miraculous.

Faith keeps us attuned to God and out of fear. It focuses us on seeing what He's doing in our lives and in the world around us. We see beyond the present circumstances and know that God will work it all out for good, even if the immediate results are not apparent. This is going beyond merely believing that God is, to steadfastly trusting Him with the intricacies of our life.

How much of what we do is really motivated by an implicit trust in God? When storms arise, either within or around you, do you immediately think of asking God to show you a way out? Do you declare to Him your plan to trust His heart to work it out in His time and chosen manner? Or are your first thoughts on how to intervene, to make something happen by your own methods? If you lose your job, do you immediately trust in your education and skill level to land you another, or do you turn to God and ask Him to provide?

The answers to these and similar questions speak to the more basic question of whether or not we're living by faith. If you're disobedient because you feel justified in believing your circumstances are worse than those of others, ask yourself whether self-deception may be operative in your life. If it is, fear will also be present. If you aren't sure, ask the Holy Spirit to reveal whether or not you believe you have faith but are really trusting in yourself. He'll gently guide you, showing you the areas you need to hand over to Him. If this is your heart's desire, He'll teach you how to trust Him and consequently leave behind fear.

A faith that saves.

Faith is essential for salvation. Without a *measure* of faith, which itself is given to us by God, we can't even come to Christ for the salvation we need. In the fourth and fifth chapters of Romans, Paul mentions faith a dozen times. Almost all are in the context of *justification* (being made righteous) by trusting in Christ alone.

It's only by His *grace* that we receive salvation and are granted access to the hope of the glory of God. Our faith is the prerequisite to our benefiting from that grace. The all-important formula: The believer is saved by *grace, through faith*, which we receive as God's free gift. This is absolutely independent of any good works we may perform (Ephesians 2:8–9). The faith that saves has its beginning when God, of His own divine initiative, calls and leads us to repentance (John 6:44).

- "Jesus answered and said to them, 'This is the work of God, that you believe in Him whom He sent.'" (John 6:29; and Romans 2:4)

Christ guides us into all truth (John 16:7–14). The Holy Spirit stirs up our minds to knowledge, and we begin to perceive what we hadn't considered before. This, combined with the confrontation that occurs when the carnal mind is forced to choose what to do with this truth, gives birth to a living faith, a faith that works and walks in godliness.

This would never occur if God didn't first do His part. We would never find the true God or understand His gospel of the kingdom on our own. We would never be able to choose the real Jesus, our Savior, from the mass of false "christs" created in the minds of people. Not knowing what to repent of or who to seek, we would never repent.

As miraculous and powerful as God's liberation of Israel from bondage was, the breaking of our bondage to Satan, this world, and our natural nature, is that much more radical and significant. This is why Ephesians 2:8 identities *saving faith* as God's gift to us.

Israel's release from Egypt was God's doing. No matter how much His people cried out to Him, the Israelites would never have left Egypt without His miraculous intervention.

To what did God lead us that sparked this saving faith in us? He led us to His Word. We can glean a measure of faith from observing God's creation, but this faith can't save because it doesn't offer guidance, direction, or reveal God's purposes for us.

We find God's purposes and the revelation of Himself only in His Word. How, then, do we receive this faith?

- "So then faith comes by hearing, and hearing by the word of God." (Romans 10:17)

Of course this doesn't imply that all who hear the message will listen, understand, or accept it. In a practical sense, this means that we need to carefully evaluate the message that's being preached. We must invest our trust in the true God and His teachings. Be sure to ask the Holy Spirit for the wisdom and spiritual discernment necessary for detecting false teaching. Much of the difference is so subtle that, were it not for the operation of the gift of "discernment of spirits," many people claiming to be Christians would be living by false gospels.

It's the Holy Spirit's role to keep us from the deception that can so easily lead us off into tangents that might cause us to fall away. By being alert and cautious about the messages you hear, and by checking everything against the Word of God to ensure correctness, you'll guard against being led astray.

The Bible proclaims this principle from beginning to end. Adam and Eve put their trust in Satan's message rather than in God's (Genesis 3:1–6).

The children of Israel listened to Korah, Dathan, Abiram, and the two-hundred fifty leaders and later succumbed to the Moabites' appeal for them to engage in sexual license. In each case many died as a direct result (Numbers 16:1–3, 25:1–3).

After Solomon's reign, Israel followed Jeroboam's false message. Jesus Himself prophesied that many would lay claim to being the Christ and deceive the unwary.

We must choose to live by faith.

God doesn't ask us to believe His message without evidence. He presents us with an overwhelming body of proof not only that He exists, but that He's working out a grand purpose that now includes us. We wouldn't be moved to read books like this had He not personally acted to stir our minds to understand the things of His Spirit. He has given us the Holy Spirit that we might know the things of God.

When we have faith, we trust in God, believing that everything He has said and promised are true. Although we may at times feel alone in the midst of a trial, we can take great comfort in recognizing that all of our predecessors in the faith experienced the same.

The very nature of faith demands that we move beyond our comfort zone. The responsibility for making wise choices, which comes from receiving knowledge and enlightenment by trusting in God's Word, falls on us. Remember the warning and advice God gave to Israel in the days before the second generation entered the Promised Land.

- "Now what I am commanding you today is not too difficult for you or beyond your reach. It is not up in heaven, so that you have to ask, 'Who will ascend into heaven to get it and proclaim it to us so we may obey it?' Nor is it beyond the sea, so that you have to ask, 'Who will cross the sea to get it and proclaim it to us so we may obey it?' No, the word is very near you; it is in your mouth and in your heart so you may obey it. See, I set before you today life and prosperity, death and destruction. For I command you today to love the Lord your God, to walk in his ways, and to keep his commands, decrees and laws; then you will live and increase, and the Lord your God will bless you in the land you are entering to possess. But if your heart turns away and you are not obedient, and if you are drawn away to bow down to other gods and worship them, I declare to you this day that you will certainly be destroyed. You will not live long in the land you are crossing the Jordan to enter and possess. This day I call heaven and earth as witnesses against you that *I have set before you life and death, blessings and curses. Now choose life*, so that you and your children may live and that you may love the Lord your God, listen to his voice, and hold fast to him. For the Lord is your life, and he will give you many years in the land he swore to give to your fathers, Abraham, Isaac and Jacob.'" (Deuteronomy 30:11–20)

The testing of our faith.

God wants to build up your faith. Like any proud parent, He loves showing off His offspring. When we stand strong in faith, refusing to believe what we see in the earthly realm only, we're showcasing our faith and glorifying God. Our Abba, our proud papa beams in doting pride when He sees that we've learned the lessons He taught us.

Sometimes God allows the storms of life to blow our way to toughen us up, to teach us to call upon Him. Nothing in our lives is safe or secure until we place it in God's care.

The disciples were concerned for their lives when the storm suddenly burst upon them. Although several of Jesus' disciples were professional fishermen, they were totally unprepared for waves of this magnitude. Navigating this lake in a storm so extreme and unpredictable was beyond their expertise; they needed to trust Jesus for their very survival.

Storms have a way of doing this to us. They shake us out of our complacency, strip us of our self-sufficiency, and force us to turn to Jesus in our extremity. Jesus allows the storms to produce four environmental conditions in which to grow our faith in Him. Our faith grows when it is:

1. nourished,
2. acted upon,
3. tested, and
4. rewarded.

We're often slack about feeding our faith, so at times God intervenes to put that faith to the test.

- "These have come so that the proven genuineness of your faith—of greater worth than gold, which perishes even though refined by fire—may result in praise, glory and honor when Jesus Christ is revealed." (1 Peter 1:7)

When God tests our faith, we're forced to put that faith to work, to exercise it, to flex our spiritual muscle in a way we might not otherwise do. We learn to dig in and hold fast to Christ as the winds howl around us threatening to pull us from His grasp. By hanging on for dear life we can weather these storms and emerge stronger for the experience.

The "hanging on" process develops our spiritual grit and stamina, motivating us to take further steps to feed and exercise our faith. We build up our endurance through life's ravages by remaining securely within the faith—and this is rewarded by God with His continued and repeated provision and rescue. Such storms incrementally build our character and prepare us for still greater tempests.

- "Perseverance must finish its work so that you may be mature and complete, not lacking anything." (James 1:3–4)

Perseverance will be needed to complete God's purposes for us. When it's time for God to move us to the next level we'll need resolve and determination. For with every promotion come increasing persecution and obstacles to hinder our trust and faith in Him.

Without perseverance at work, we'll easily give up at the first instance of criticism instead of praise. Or when, Satan tempts us with the message that the task is just too difficult—too much hard work and not enough reward.

Storms are also permitted to come upon us so we can be helpful to others. If we never go through a raging torrent, we'll never develop empathy for others in their times of need. A sheltered, storm-free existence keeps us complacent and self-focused, hardly the selfless life to which Christ has called us. There would be no need for us to put up with others, nor would we need the give-and-take of family or other relationships, if this were the way the Lord intended us to live. We would have no need, either, of a relationship with Him.

God created us exactly the way He wants us—social beings in need of fellowship, relationship, intimacy, and desire for Him.

As part of our natural sociability, we're to share God's good news with others. Storms help us to feel compassion for the lost and hurting. They instill urgency within us to share with others how to be free from life's inevitable suffering and fear.

Prayer produces in us a peace that transcends our ability to explain or comprehend (Philippians 4:7). This unfathomable peace guards our hearts and minds even in extreme adversity.

Paul was able to write about the peace of the Lord from prison. He understood firsthand about harsh environments and cruelty from others. Most of us will never face anything like what the apostle Paul endured. Nevertheless, he was capable of experiencing the most beautiful serenity and peace in the midst of horrible conditions. What a testimony to all believers. Surely if he could find reasons to rejoice in spite of such hardships, we can do the same.

- "Rejoice in the Lord always. I will say it again: Rejoice! Let your gentleness be evident to all. The Lord is near. Do not be anxious about anything, but in every situation, by prayer and petition, with thanksgiving, present your requests to God. And the peace of God, which transcends all understanding, will guard your hearts and your minds in Christ Jesus. Finally, brothers and sisters, whatever is true, whatever is noble, whatever is right, whatever is pure, whatever is lovely, whatever is admirable—if anything is excellent or praiseworthy—think about such things. Whatever you have learned or received or heard from me, or seen in me—put it into practice. And the God of peace will be with you." (Philippians 4:4–9)

What an excellent model for how we're to come before our God in prayer. Praying in this manner changes our very nature and heart. We receive in response a heart that's soft toward God, and we begin to see and hear what He wants to give us. We start to believe without doubt and wavering.

Be sure to come to God with your prayers in *belief*. Sometimes we come to the Lord in stiffness or skepticism. If we approach Him in a formal way, relying solely on written or repetitious prayers that aren't spoken from our heart in intimacy with Him, we'll find the experience of praying empty or mechanical. Approaching God at arm's length in a spirit of doubt or challenge, will keep us in fear. Fear will never allow us to move toward God in faith, love, and devotion—as He desires.

Be sure to thank God in and through the storms He's allowing in your life, rather than continuously questioning Him about your troubles. Unfortunately, much of our growth comes about while we in the crucible of pain. You don't need to be thankful for the storms themselves, but for what they are producing in you—perseverance.

Problems work to perfect us for God's higher calling and purpose. Be sure to be mindful in the *midst* of these storms, that God is perfecting you through them. Difficulties produce for us a greater appreciation of what Jesus went through on our behalf. They construct a more intimate, trusting relationship and a mellowed maturity and a heightened capacity to understand and appreciate His person. This changes the depth and quality of your relationship with Him—and that's a beautiful thing to acquire.

We lose heart if we don't understand what God is accomplishing in and through our difficulties. He's in the process of making us *complete*. This is how strong faith is developed. Be sure to take Him up on His offer; don't question or turn from Him at the hint of difficulty. Your life will be the better for it. Trusting in our Savior gives us the proper perspective we need to see our way out of living a fear-filled life.

Accept Jesus and His methods of working in your life. In doing so you will live an abundant, overflowing life filled with hope, joy, peace, gratitude, and maturity. Be sure to praise Him and thank Him for saving you and for keeping you in His perfect peace.

6

SHE WORSHIPS GOD
IN SPIRIT AND IN TRUTH

"And God required worship as directed by His Word."
(Deuteronomy 5:32-33)

In these last days Satan is doing all he can to deceive God's children and incite them to compromise their faith. Yet, the Bible tells us that if we'll worship God according to His commands—*in Spirit* and *in truth*—that we won't be deceived by the evil one.

Spiritual matters are often confusing. Without discernment our understanding is naturally cloudy. We're continually viewing godly things through the faulty lens of our natural senses. We have such limited clarity when it comes to spiritual truth that we're in need of continual illumination. This enlightenment comes from the Holy Spirit, as He makes the complex understandable to us.

The vast majority of people today have received little training regarding the subject of worship and most aren't aware that God has a say in how we are to worship Him. Countless people choose churches based on the type of music and preaching they like to hear. Most believe they have the prerogative of worshiping God in any manner they choose, or worse, opting not to worship Him at all.

But the Bible clearly contradicts this notion that we get to choose our mode of worship.

Our salvation is serious business and it won't occur by accident. God tells that our salvation must be *worked out* "with fear and trembling"

(Philippians 2:12). Returning thanks and praise to God through worship is essential to our salvation.

God desires our worship as He's the only One worthy of it. To *worship* means "to give honor, reverence, respect, adoration, praise, and glory to a superior being." Our worship acknowledges His greatness, power, and glory, and He is pleased and glorified when we do so.

- "You are **worthy**, our Lord and God, to receive **glory** and **honor** and **power, for you created all things**, and by your will they were created and have their being." (Revelation 4:11)

- "You shall not make for yourself an idol in the form of anything in heaven above or on the earth beneath or in the waters below. You shall not bow down to them or worship them; for I, the Lord your God, am a jealous God, punishing the children for the sin of the fathers to the third and fourth generation of those who hate me." (Deuteronomy 5:8–9)

These verses tell us what God thinks about the matter of worship. He also lets us know what He thinks about our giving worship to "idols" (other things or people) rather than to Him. Idols are never worthy of our praise or adoration; they hold no value and have no ability to create, as our God does. God takes very seriously our desire to place our worship elsewhere.

Worship provokes us to reflect on the majesty and graciousness of God the Father, Jesus, and the Holy Spirit. Their majesty reveals to us, in contrast, our own unworthiness.

God is not in *need* of our worship. But we give it to *please* Him. Acts of worship, such as singing, praying, and studying His Word, are designed by God to bring us closer to Him. They motivate us to become more like Him.

God's jealousy isn't the sinful envy born of pride that people experience. It's a holy, righteous, tenacious jealousy that demands glorification by His creation.

What is the purpose of our worship?

The purpose of worship is to glorify, honor, praise, exalt, and please our heavenly Father. Our worship reflects our adoration and loyalty in return for God's grace and mercy. The nature of the worship God desires is *humble* and *contrite submission*. Worship involves giving sincere and earnest respect, love, esteem, and adulation to the One who gave us our being.

- "God resists the proud, but gives grace to the humble. *Humble yourselves in the sight of the Lord*, and He will lift you up." (James 4:6, 10)

- "God who made the world and everything in it, since He is Lord of heaven and earth, does not dwell in temples made with hands. Nor is He worshiped with men's hands, as though He needed anything, since He gives life, breath, and all things." (Acts 17:24–25)

How do we take on the mind of Christ?

We renew our mind as we study and meditate on God's Word and worship Him *only*. Our worship not only honors and magnifies God, but edifies and restores us as well. When we worship God, we come to value what He values and gradually take on His characteristics and qualities. As Christians we're called to become Christ-like, to conform ourselves to His image.

- "And *do not be conformed to this world*, but *be transformed by the renewing of your mind*." (Romans 12:2)

- "Draw near to God and He will draw near to you." (James 4:8)

- "Let this mind be in you which was also in Christ." (Philippians 2:5)

When we worship God, our mind is being renewed and conformed. A mind conformed to Christ has forgiveness, gentleness, compassion, virtue, purity, kindness, and love. This prepares us to live with God while on earth, but also in heaven for all eternity.

- "Set your mind on things above and not on things on the earth." (Colossians 3:2)

Does Scripture give us the latitude to decide whether and how we'll worship God?

Authentic worship isn't about what we want to do, but what God wants us to do according to His Word. The ritual of faithfully going to church every week doesn't guarantee that a person is worshipping God. John gives us clear instruction on how we're to conduct ourselves in worship:

- Jesus said, "But an hour is coming, and now is, when the true worshipers will worship the Father in spirit and truth; for such people the Father seeks to be His worshipers. God is spirit, and those who worship Him must worship in spirit and truth." (John 4:23–24, NASB)

What does it mean to worship God in Spirit and in truth?

Worshiping God "*in spirit*" means with reverence, attentiveness, understanding, and the appropriate purpose of honoring God. Our worship must reflect His glory.

- "Let us have grace, by which we may serve God acceptably with reverence and godly fear. For our God is a consuming fire." (Hebrews 12:28–29)
- "For you were bought with a price; therefore glorify God in your body and in your spirit, which are God's." (1 Corinthians 6:20)

Worship goes much deeper than singing songs and reciting written prayers. The fact that the Bible tells us how to worship, indicates that most of us know little about how or why we're to do it. God's instructions to us are always for our benefit. He wants only the very best for His children. Worship is part of living to the full. If we want to please our heavenly Father we must learn everything we can about how He wants us to worship Him.

God teaches us all things through the Holy Spirit, including the capacity to love and worship Him as He desires. We can't understand or please God without His power operating in us.

Jesus teaches that the place of our worship is of no consequence to God. It doesn't matter whether we're in a home, a tent, or in a stadium. The location of our worship has nothing to do with whether that worship is acceptable to God.

The woman at the well.

The context of John 4:23–24 is a discussion between Jesus and a woman at a village well. She correctly recognizes Jesus as a prophet and asks him a question regarding the appropriate place to worship God.

Jesus reminds her that since she is a Samaritan, she can't have been taught the truth about the worship of God. Notice the contrast here between the "true worshipers" and the Samaritans, who followed their own traditions rather than the Word of God.

God expects us to worship Him as an expression of our reverence and thanksgiving. But the Lord desires more than that. He's looking for our deep devotion and desire to please Him. Our devotion signifies our love and is demonstrated by our obedience.

God requires not only hearers of the Word, but doers as well. Those who long to please and honor God by their obedience, reflect the difference between those who are merely called and those who are chosen.

The parable of the wedding feast and what it means for us.

- "For many are called, but few are chosen." (Matthew 22:14, NKJV)

Since this Scripture is confusing to many, let's examine it. This statement concludes the parable of the wedding feast, which Jesus told to show what the kingdom of heaven will be like when the end of the age comes. In this parable the king sends out his servants to gather guests for the wedding feast.

But those invited refuse to come, some because they're supposedly too busy with their worldly pursuits, and others because they're hostile toward the king.

So the king commands his servants to go out and invite anyone they meet, resulting in a huge influx of willing and eager guests filling the wedding hall. The king, spotting one man without the proper wedding garments, sends him away. Jesus clarifies that although many are called or invited into the kingdom, only those who have been chosen and have received Christ will indeed come. Those who try to enter without the covering of the blood of Christ are inadequately clothed and will be cast into "outer darkness," signifying hell.

- "Then the king said to the servants, 'Bind him hand and foot, take him away, and cast him into outer darkness; there will be weeping and gnashing of teeth.'" (Matthew 22:13)

What does this mean? Many people hear the call of God. It comes through His revelation of Himself through His creation and through our conscience. But relatively few will respond or tune their ears to hear and listen when God speaks to them.

- Jesus said many times, "He who has ears to hear, let him hear." (Matthew 11:15; Mark 4:9; and Luke 8:8, 14:35)

Everyone has ears, but only a few really listen and respond unwaveringly. Not everyone who hears the gospel receives it, but only the few who are earnestly seeking and receptive to the Good News.

This usually occurs within those who recognize and acknowledge a yearning or emptiness within themselves and seek to find the remedy for their condition. This yearning for something more comes from God. We can't claim the initiative, since God must draw the hearts of those who will come.

The masses who hear demonstrate little or no interest and many manifest outright antagonism towards God. Yet, God longs to bring them in. Countless are called or invited into the kingdom, even though God knows they will not respond favorably to His calling.

- "No one can come to me unless the Father who sent me draws him, and I will raise him up at the last day." (John 6:44)

God not only wants us to love Him as He has first loved us; but He wants us to take it a step further. He wants us to act justly toward others with love and compassion. We bring Him glory as we become a living sacrifice, holy and pleasing. (Romans 12:1).

God creates life, grants forgiveness, and fills us with faith. People are completely unable without the Holy Spirit's intervention, to do the things necessary to enter the kingdom of heaven.

- "For he chose us in him before the creation of the world to be holy and blameless in his sight. In love he predestined us to be adopted as his sons through Jesus Christ, in accordance with his pleasure and will—to the praise of his glorious grace, which he has freely given us in the One he loves." (Ephesians 1:4–6)

Salvation is by God's will and pleasure and for His glory.

All of God's "chosen," without exception, will come to salvation. Each of them will hear and respond, because God's power makes certain they've been given spiritual ears to hear the truth.

- "All that the Father gives me will come to me, and whoever comes to me I will never drive away. For I have come down from heaven not to do my will but to do the will of him who sent me. And this is the will of him who sent me, that I shall lose none of all that he has given me, but raise them up at the last day. . . . No one can come to me unless the Father who sent me draws him, and I will raise him up at the last day. It is written in the Prophets: 'They will all be taught by God.' Everyone who listens to the Father and learns from him comes to me." (John 6:37-39, 44-45)

- "And we know that in all things God works for the good of those who love him, who have been called according to his purpose. For those God foreknew (loved) he also predestined to be conformed to the likeness of his Son, that he might be the firstborn among many brothers. And those he predestined, he also called; those he called, he also justified; those he justified, he also glorified." (Romans 8:28–30)

- "Therefore, if anyone is in Christ, he is a new creation; the old has gone, the new has come." (2 Corinthians 5:17)

How do we know whether we're among the few who've been given ears to hear?

By responding to the call! Our assurance comes to us from the Holy Spirit. If we listen with our spiritual ears and respond to the invitation, we'll experience inner, reverential fear as we recognize God's work in us to bring about our salvation.

- "...being confident of this, that he who began a good work in you will carry it on to completion until the day of Christ Jesus." (Philippians 1:6)

- "Therefore, my dear friends, as you have always obeyed—not only in my presence, but now much more in my absence—continue to work out your salvation with fear and trembling, for it is God who works in you to will and to act according to his good purpose." (Philippians 2:12–13)

Elements of true worship.

When we worship with an obedient heart and an open and repentant spirit, God is glorified, other Christians are purified, the Church is edified, and the lost are evangelized. God commands our worship because our eternal destiny depends on our willingness to worship the true and living God.

The book of Philippians describes the true Church—the body of believers in Jesus Christ whose eternal destiny is heaven.

- "For we are the circumcision, who worship God in the spirit, and rejoice in Christ Jesus, and have no confidence in the flesh." (Philippians 3:3)

These are all elements of true worship. The Church is made up of those who worship God in their spirit, rejoice in Christ, and refuse to trust in themselves or in their own works for salvation.

Those who decline to worship the true and living God don't belong to Him. Their eternal destiny is hell. True worshipers are identified by the act of worship, and their eternal home is with the God they adore.

God both demands and deserves our worship, and it's natural to the nature of true Christians to worship Him.

The mark of a true Christian—a circumcised heart.

The Church is uniquely identified as the full assembly of God's people. We aren't identified by physical circumcision as in the Old Testament, but by the circumcision of our heart. A pure heart is a single-minded heart. The number one aim of a Christian's life is to know and pursue God.

So what constitutes a circumcised heart? *Circumcision* means "a cutting away." A circumcised heart is a heart that's willing to rid itself of anything that threatens to crowd out God. That includes aspects of our lives that may be good and even necessary, for the good is often the enemy of the best. A Christian with a circumcised heart understands that good works can never serve as a means of salvation, for only Jesus' works were sinless and sufficient for that. They understand that no amount of human effort can earn them anything. Salvation is a free gift from God made available to us by grace (His) through faith (our humble and thankful response to that grace).

- "For it is by grace you have been saved, through faith—and this not from yourselves, it is the gift of God—not by works, so that no one can boast." (Ephesians 2:8–9)

Spiritual worship has two components.

1. *Worshiping in spirit.* To worship God in spirit means that our worship comes from our heart. Pure worship is attentive, earnest, and genuine. It's free from insincerity, distractions, and selfishness. Formal rituals aren't a substitute. Religious rituals come from our outward being rather than from our inward being, or "spirit." Spirit worship results from our spirit being one with God's. When we're separated from God, we substitute worship with works of religion. True worship comes from those whose minds are centered on the magnificence of the incomparable and only God.

2. *Worshiping in truth.* We must additionally worship God in truth. Regardless of how sincere a person may be, if her worship is not in truth, according to the Truth as contained in God's Word, it will be unacceptable to Him.

The written Word provides specific instructions on how to worship God. If we add to what the Scripture tells us, or subtract from it, our attempted worship will be in vain. This was the problem of the Samaritans.

False worshipers believe their own thoughts are more important than God's. True worshipers simply want to glorify God. Unless we look to God's Word regarding true worship, we'll make the same mistake the Samaritans made in Jesus' day—which is worshipping God in ignorance.

- "Sanctify them by the truth; *your word is truth.*" (John 17:17)
- "But as He who called you is holy, you also be holy in your conduct, because it is written, Be holy for I am holy." (1 Peter 1:15–16)
- Jesus said, "Isaiah was right when he prophesied about you hypocrites; as it is written: 'These people honor me with their lips, but their hearts are far from me.'" (Mark 7:6)

When our heart is right toward God, we willingly and joyfully participate in worship. True worshipers find worship a time of joy, a time of drinking in the love and unconditional acceptance their Savior has for them.

We are spirit—as God is spirit.

God's Spirit lives in all true believers. In fact, Scripture tells us that when we take that first step of belonging to God through Christ—we are one with Him in spirit.

- "The Spirit himself testifies with our spirit that we are God's children." (Romans 8:16, NIV)
- Or, as rendered in the NLT: "For his Spirit joins with our spirit to affirm that we are God's children." (Romans 8:16)
- "We have not received the spirit of the world but the Spirit who is from God, that we may understand what God has freely given us." (1 Corinthians 2:12)

In the story of the rich man and Lazarus recorded in Luke 16:19–30, we see that the human spirit has consciousness apart from the body.

The rich man could *remember* and *feel* while in Hades (hell). His body was in the grave, but his inner man, his spirit, was capable of all the thoughts, memories, and emotions of conscience life.

The essence of life is spirit—and God is Spirit.

Since God is a spirit, He is both invisible and immaterial, and He requires worship of a similar nature. In other words, He requires "spiritual worship," not material worship.

- "Among those who approach me I will be proved holy; in the sight of all the people I will be honored." (Leviticus 10:3)

As a spirit, God is also a person we can know personally. God is not an inanimate object. Pagan idols, on the other hand, are obviously inanimate, fashioned by people. There's nothing supernatural about them. Our idols of today may differ from the pagan idols in the Old Testament, but never the less, we make many worldly *things* our idols. Yet, our lifeless idols don't respond to us, while our relational God certainly does.

God does what no idol can do. Before we had even turned from sin toward Him, while we were still *in* our sin, God was already showing His compassion toward us. God sent His Son to die on our behalf so we wouldn't die needlessly in our sin. This God did for us out of pure, unconditional, no-strings-attached love.

No idol can do that for you. Idols won't love you, die for you, or take away your sin and remember it no more. These inconceivable blessings are promises that God gave to humanity. Those who believe and trust Him on the basis of these promises will live with Him forever in a glorified state.

Jesus is alive! The very word *spirit* means "breath," and breath is the evidence of life. Throughout Scripture Jesus is called the living God. An impersonal force or idol doesn't speak to people or give them logical directions.

- "My soul yearns, even faints, for the courts of the Lord; my heart and my flesh cry out for the living God." (Psalm 84:2)
- "...for they themselves report what kind of reception you gave us. They tell how you turned to God from idols to serve the living and true God." (1 Thessalonians 1:9)
- He told Moses that His name was, "I am who I am" (Exodus 3:14).

God has personality.

God has the basic characteristics of personality—intellect, emotions, and will. He thinks, feels, and acts. And that's good news! Since He's a living person, we can get to know Him personally and communicate with Him freely. If He were an impersonal force, there would be no hope of intimacy with Him.

How do we go about glorifying God in our worship?

In the Old Testament the word *glory*, as it relates to God, means greatness of splendor. While in the New Testament the word translated *glory* means dignity, honor, praise, or worship. Putting the two together, we find that glorifying God means acknowledging His greatness, a greatness that demands our attributing to Him honor and glory through our praise and worship. God's glory is the essence of His nature, and we give Him glory by acknowledging that essence.

- "I must be glorified." (Leviticus 10:3, NKJV)

If God already has all the glory, which He does, then how do we *give* Him glory? How can we give God something that's His in the first place? The explanation is found in 1 Chronicles.

- "Ascribe to the Lord, O families of nations, ascribe to the Lord *glory* and strength, ascribe to the Lord the *glory due his name*.

Bring an offering and come before him; ***worship the Lord*** in the splendor of his holiness." (1 Chronicles 16:28–29)

We see that two components together make up the action of glorifying God.

1.   We ascribe, or "give," glory to God because it's His due.

2.   No one else deserves the praise and worship we offer up to Him.

We're to *bring an offering* to God as part of our *act of worship*. The only acceptable offering we can bring, as we come before Him in the beauty of His holiness, consists of agreement, obedience, submission, rehearsing His attributes, and extolling Him. Glorifying God begins with concurring with everything He says, especially about Himself.

- "I am the Lord; that is my name! I will not give my glory to another or my praise to idols." (Isaiah 42:8)

- "I am the Lord God. I created the heavens like an open tent above. I made the earth and everything that grows on it. I am the source of life for all who live on this earth, so listen to what I say." (Isaiah 42:5)

Because God is holy, perfect, and true, His proclamations of Himself are completely true (Psalm 19:7). We glorify God by proclaiming, acknowledging, and rehearsing what is true, back to Him.

God's Word holds His truth—all we need for life is in Him. Listening to and agreeing with Him, though, won't glorify Him unless we also submit to Him by obeying the commands contained in His Word.

- "But from everlasting to everlasting the Lord's love is with those who fear him, and his righteousness with their children's children—with those who keep his covenant and remember to obey his precepts." (Psalm 103:17–18)

Jesus repeated that glorifying and loving God are one and the same.

- "If you love me, you will obey what I command." (John 14:15)

In his final sermon before he was martyred for his faith, Stephen retold the story of God's dealings with Israel from the time Abraham left his country in obedience to God's command, to the coming of Christ.

God receives glory when we proclaim to others His marvelous attributes and deeds, when we share how He saved us from the snares of sin and how He has changed our heart, mind, emotions, and entire life—we bring Him glory!

It doesn't matter that others may not receive our message. God is glorified when we proclaim it nevertheless. He'll see to it that the message reaches those who have ears to hear and will eventually come.

The crowd that heard Stephen hated what he said, so much so that they picked up stones to kill him.

- "But Stephen, full of the Holy Spirit, looked up to heaven and saw the glory of God, and Jesus standing at the right hand of God." (Acts 7:55)

To glorify God is to extol His attributes, among them His holiness, faithfulness, mercy, grace, love, majesty, sovereignty, power, and omniscience. When others can see these same virtues working in us, we testify to the power of God to change lives. This brings Him glory!

Cain and Abel's attitude towards worship.

God set the standard of worship already through the children of Adam and Eve, Cain and Abel. After God told these two young men what was pleasing to Him, we see that God accepted Abel's *offering* and *worship*, but rejected Cain's. (Genesis 4:1–15).

These two children of the same parents had dispositions that differed in every way. They had diverse gifts and abilities, which lead them to different occupations; not a problem in itself. One becomes a farmer and the other a shepherd. But these brothers differed in an eternally significant way as well—they diverged radically in terms of their *moral character.*

Cain developed wicked traits. On the positive side, he was energetic, ambitious, resourceful, a man who made his mark in the world, a builder of cities, a leader in civilization, but he was also a man of bad temper, selfish, cruel, hardened, and resentful. Cain wanted to become a self-made man, perhaps one who would become rich, powerful, and determine his own future—one who would answer to no one.

Abel, in contrast, we picture as docile, sensitive, affectionate, patient, meek, and humble in spirit. The kind of man described in the Beatitudes as poor in spirit, hungering and thirsting after righteousness, merciful, a

103

peacemaker, bearing wrong without complaint and declining to strive for control. Abel determined to let God make him into the man He wanted him to become. He was humble before the Lord, not insistent upon directing his own way.

Both brothers worshiped God.

Both were worshipers of God, though in this area too, they were opposites. Cain brought of the fruit of the ground for his offering, while Abel brought the firstlings of his flock. Perhaps Cain may have failed to contribute the first or best of his yield. Some suppose that Cain's offering was unfit in itself, inferring that God had already instituted the offering of blood as the only acceptable worship. We don't know this, but we know from the account that the Lord had respect for Abel and his offering, but not for Cain and his offering.

Abel most likely gave willingly and joyfully, while Cain gave grudgingly, from a sense of duty with little gratitude in his heart. Cain wouldn't have become bitter over God's rebuke if his attitude toward God had been right to begin with. Instead he would have returned with a more suitable offering and corrected the problem (though that faith in God would have kept him from bringing an unacceptable offering in the first place).

Here we catch a glimpse not just of the offering, but of the heart that offered it. This is vital to helping us understand what God looks for and finds acceptable in His people.

The primary difference between Cain and Abel.

The real lesson for us isn't God's rejection or acceptance, but the fact that Cain rejected God, while Abel accepted Him.

In the epistle to the Hebrews we're told that it was Abel's *faith* that made his sacrifice more excellent than Cain's. We learn from this account that God must be worshiped in the way He commands, and that worship is serious business to Him. We learn too that the acceptance of our worship depends on our heart when we offer it. Cain's heart was wrong, while Abel's was right. God cares nothing about the forms of worship; He looks into the heart and is pleased when He finds there love, faith, and true devotion.

Cain didn't offer his sacrifice by faith, therefore he didn't worship according to the Word of God. As a result, his offering was rejected.

Abel, on the other hand, offered his sacrifice by faith. He heard and obeyed the Word of God (Hebrews 11:4).

Cain was arrogant and presumptuous.

We can immediately discern Cain's underlying problem: he'd lost, or perhaps had never found, "the fear of the Lord."

Anger tends to make us arrogant, believing from the outset that we have the right to be angry. Anger goes hand in hand with pride and deceit, disabling our ability to perceive our own bias in a matter. Pride is fatal, for it was pride that led to Satan's defeat.

Cain's rebellious attitude and actions demonstrated that he thought he had the right to substitute his own judgment for God's. The *way of Cain* is the way of presumption.

Those who neglect God's clear teaching in matters of salvation, are demonstrating the attitude of Cain. The simple truth is that God will not tolerate such audacity.

- "Keep your servant also from willful sins; may they not rule over me. Then I will be blameless, innocent of great transgression." (Psalm 19:13)

Cain was angry with God.

Why was Cain angry? Was his rage at God for not showing respect for his offering? Did he think God had spurned him for no good reason? If he was irate against God, how foolish. What good does it do to become angry with God? To whom else can we turn?

It's ridiculous for people to direct their anger and rage against God, although countless do just that. Ingratitude for all God does for us, or the inability or unwillingness to see that all good things come from Him, makes one unthankful and arrogant.

Many fail to recognize that all they are and own is based on the goodness of God who gives us our very breath for life. How foolish to fault the Creator Himself, to allow ourselves to become angry at Him. This is the first sign that iniquity has gripped our heart and made us thankless.

Cain was angry with Abel—simply because Abel was good.

When Cain ceased being thankful, conceit cracked open the door to his heart and permitted pride to enter.

Evil hates both God and good, and won't tolerate people who demonstrate their love for God by doing good. Countless innocent Christians have been persecuted for no other reason than that they were good and loved God. The root of Cain's anger was jealousy. The fruit brought forth from it was murder and the consequent expulsion from the land by God.

Pride invariably produces alienation from God, as well as the end of all the good blessings humility brings to us. Envy is a contemptible passion, breeding evil upon evil. Devastation is never far behind when pride appears.

Repentance will free us from arrogance and pride.

Repentance is the only means by which we can be washed clean by the blood of Jesus. It liberates us from our bent toward carnality and evil. The stories in the Bible were written for our admonishment. They caution us what to turn from. The danger of cherishing even the smallest beginning of bitterness is that we never know into what it will grow.

Many make light of their bad temper, attributing it to a character trait inherited from a family member. But we see in the account of Cain and Abel that a quick temper is anything but a harmless weakness.

In His reproof of Cain, the Lord likens his sin to a wild beast lurking behind his door, ready to leap on and devour him. This is true of all sin that we entertain in our heart. It may lie dormant and seemingly harmless for a long time, but it's only a wild beast sleeping.

- "You will be accepted if you do what is right. But if you refuse to do what is right, then watch out! Sin is crouching at the door, eager to control you. But you must subdue it and be its master." (Genesis 4:7, NLT)

So it is with the passions and lusts of the old nature that we have ignored and allowed to nest in our heart. They'll crouch there waiting, until in some unguarded hour they rise up in all their viciousness.

Cain's resentment grew into unbridled anger. Cain refused to rebuke or repent of his anger, and it quickly grew into a furious, uncontrollable passion.

- "It came to pass when they were in the field, that Cain attacked his brother Abel and killed him!" (Genesis 4:8).

All sin, if ignored and allowed to dwell within us, grows into more devastating sin. It was the apostle John who stated that "He who hates his brother is a murderer" (1 John 3:15). John remarks further that the one who hates a brother or sister is a liar.

It's interesting and sad how one sin can lead to another. Hatred is a seed, a seed that, when it grows into its full force, can even manifest itself in murder.

Guard yourself against envy.

We need to be continually on guard against envy. Few other sins are more common or more deadly. How easily we become jealous when we perceive someone else to be more gifted or capable, or when we focus on the reality that someone has more possessions or a higher position than we do. People every day are murdered because someone permitted themselves to be overcome by covetousness and anger.

Envy is included among the "seven deadly sins." It has been noted that of these seven sins, envy most disturbs our peace of mind. We must guard against the first inklings of resentment if we hope to escape its snare.

It was only after Cain had committed his crime that he allowed himself to think of its enormity. God asked rhetorically, "What have you done? Your brother's blood cries out to Me from the ground!"

People don't stop to think beforehand of the consequence of the evil they contemplate. They're carried away by passion for pleasure, power, or gain, to the point that they don't see the darkness of the deed they're about to commit. But when it's done and they turn around to gaze at it, they see it in all its ugliness.

If we would stop to assess the probable consequences first, before committing a crime or an act of disobedience towards God, to discern the end before the beginning, we could save ourselves and others from so much heartache and pain. In a moment, in a frenzied fit of unrestrained emotion, we can lose everything based on our failure to heed God's warning to be self-controlled.

Giving God all glory through our worship.

Our spirit was planted in us as a means of connecting to God's indwelling Spirit. Those who are Holy Spirit filled are able to discern the truth contained in God's Word. God desires to direct our steps and to enjoy relationship with us. Worship is part of that relationship through fellowship.

Satan, the god of this world, wants nothing more than the church to incorporate worldly elements into their worship. When we're inclined toward compromise in our worship, that worship will reflect the world.

- "The god of this age has blinded the minds of unbelievers, so that they cannot see the light of the gospel that displays the glory of Christ, who is the image of God." (2 Corinthians 4:4).

Worship comes naturally to those who recognize God as the only source of good in a sin-filled world. Maintaining that fellowship isn't always easy, for we bring into the relationship the traditions of our upbringing and our past. But as believers we're called to move beyond our traditions, to receive with an open mind and heart the truth God's Word holds for us.

Jesus honored God by fulfilling His purpose on earth. We honor God in the same way. When we, with our whole heart, pursue God and what He has for us, we fulfill our purpose. This brings God glory.

We bring God glory when we worship Him with sincere love, honor, devotion, and a deep sense of gratitude. Tears come naturally when we focus on our loving Father and what He has done to change us. Worship is more than praising, singing, and praying to God. Worship is a lifestyle of enjoying God. When we surrender our life to Him freely, we give Him glory. Respect and reverence comes from a devoted heart, and is our act of worship.

When we love others as God commands, we bring Him glory. When we choose to set our differences aside, and learn to act out our love, we show the world we've been transformed by God's love towards us. This brings God glory.

When we die to self and become more Christ-like as a result, we bring God glory. Spiritual maturity is becoming like Jesus in the way we think and act. The more we develop Christ's character, the more we bring God glory.

When we desire to serve others with our spiritual gifts, rather than being served, we bring God glory. Our gifts have been given to us to edify the church. Growing into spiritual maturity and then sharing the good news with others as a result of that growth, brings God glory.

Acts of devotion and service are practical forms of our worship. Glorifying God with our lives should be our established lifestyle. Right worship profoundly transforms us and is one indicator that our nature has changed.

Worship comes easily to those who feel a deep sense of gratitude to God for all His tender care and love. This is the heart of worship. And this glories our God!

Conclusion

As I mentioned several times in this book *faith is an **action** word.* Faith requires you to do something with the knowledge you receive.

My prayer for you is that you turn from your past and look to Jesus for your new and better future. If you do not know Jesus personally, you can start your new journey by becoming acquainted:

Prayer of Salvation:

Jesus, I know that you are the only way to a new life. I know that you died for me because you love me and want me with you for all eternity. I accept your love and invite you into my life to be my personal Savior and Lord. Change me and mold me into your likeness. Help me to live for you and to produce good fruit for the rest of my life.

Thank you for the gift of the Holy Spirit. Holy Spirit I invite you to do an astounding, transforming work in my life.

Thank you Lord Jesus for your sacrifice, grace, and mercy. Amen

You may contact Lilliet at: *lilliet1@hotmail.com*

END NOTES

Chapter 1

1. By Dr. Charles Stanley/articles/The Value of Weakness/intouch.org)

Chapter 3

1. The Life Application Bible, NIV, *Introduction to Ruth.*
1. Walter A. Elwell, ed., Baker's Bible Handbook, p. 166.
2. Article copyrighted © 1999, Glen Hopkins.
3. Mike Murdock, "*The Proverbs 31 Woman,*" Wisdom International; Published 1/1/1994.

Chapter 4

1. http://www.gci.org/bible/1peter3, by Michael Morrison.
2. Bible-knowledge.com/fruits-of-the-holy-spirit.

Chapter 5

1. *The Fear Factor*, Psalm 27, message notes by Dr. Mark Platt.
2. "*Wandering in the Wilderness,*" Forerunner, "Personal," July 1995, by John W. Ritenbaugh.